The Entrepreneur's Guide

Deaver Brown

The Entrepreneur's Guide

MACMILLAN PUBLISHING CO., INC.

New York

COLLIER MACMILLAN PUBLISHERS

London

Macmillan Publishing Co., Inc.
866 Third Avenue, New York, N.Y. 10022
Collier Macmillan Canada, Ltd.

Library of Congress Cataloging in Publication Data

Brown, Deaver.
The entrepreneur's guide.

Bibliography: p.
Includes index.
1. Business. 2. Entrepreneur. 3. New business enterprises. I. Title.
HF5351.B8457   1980   658.1'141   80-459
ISBN 0-02-517360-X

FIRST PRINTING 1980
Designed by Jack Meserole
Printed in the United States of America

To Judy

Contents

vii

5

Sales 86

6

Finance 103

7

Operations 128

8

Professionals and the Business Environment 150

9

Conclusion 160

CONTENTS

Preface

Entrepreneurs are becoming a dying race in America. They seem to be throwbacks to less regulated eras when institutions and laws held less sway. During those periods of economic upheaval, new ventures prospered and appeared to be the surest route to financial security and personal happiness. The most able business people ventured away from salaried jobs and founded new enterprises to secure their futures.

Multinational corporations have changed all that. Now the status and security offered by huge companies are the very deterrents to new venture careers. Young people of even average ability are gobbled up by the Fortune 500 companies. The employment bait is professional status, high starting salaries, generous fringe benefits, and secure futures. Living standards rise quickly to meet these high compensation levels; futures appear protected by visions of promotions, pension plans, and sugarplums.

Young managers gradually become locked into these comfortable life-styles and find that, by the time bureaucratic fatigue and boredom set in, they are much like indentured servants of the corporation. Large mortgages, car payments, and installment loans seem to offer compelling reasons to stick with the solid job. Little wonder that so many young executives look thirty, but sound sixty-five!

This book was written to assist you in escaping an early death by job boredom. The first chapter will help you evaluate an entrepreneurial career by comparing executive and new venture life-styles, describing the necessary entrepreneurial personality traits, and outlining the risks of becoming an entrepreneur. The other chapters provide a survival kit for founding your own business and making it work. Above all, they will tell you what to expect should you choose to venture away from the norm and become an entrepreneur.

Acknowledgments

Alex Goodwin, my old friend and Cross River partner, deserves special recognition for his business judgment, perseverance, and inspiration. I would also like to thank the following people for having given me support and faith when it really counted: Dorothy Betcher, Clint Merrick, Ed Caso, Jim Sloan, Bob Majka, Harold Tananbaum, Karl Weiskopf, Bill Sites, Peter Hughes, Bob Hewitt, Ira Kipnis, Peter Van Ooosterhout, Al DiMuro, Ron Klammer, Bob Arnold, Rich Gillece, Mike Schweiger, Bob Gawlowski, Nick Soeldner, Sumner Swig, Paul Garvin, Marvin Rosenberg, Larry Sherman, and Ken Sherman. To Glenn Skwerer, Christina Rago, and Jeanne Fredericks I owe special thanks for their encouragement to finish this manuscript. And above all, I am grateful to Judy Prewitt Brown, who has endured my entrepreneurial life and done invaluable editing of this book.

The
Entrepreneur's
Guide

Getting Started

WHY BE AN ENTREPRENEUR

You should become an entrepreneur for one principal reason. It was stated most eloquently by Thomas Jefferson: *"Freedom* is the right to choose. The right to create for oneself the alternatives. Without the possibility of choice, and the exercise of choice, a man is not a man but a member, an instrument, a thing."

In a world of congested regulations, sprawling bureaucracies, and arbitrary social engineering, independent companies offer a unique freedom to their founders. They provide an escape from the petty executive concerns of office size, rank, salary levels, fringe benefits, and lunch partners. The new company presents an opportunity to do something fundamental and imaginative.

You should confront this reality before beginning your mad adventure so that you can accept the true entrepreneurial motivation without endless self-analysis and self-justification. This will permit you to get on with your personal and business life with relative peace of mind. Most entrepreneurs feel embarrassed, at least in part, by their non-money motivation. Corporate friends and neighbors endlessly discuss the monetary reasons why they work. Vacations, weekends, security, and possessions compensate for the slavery and vacancy of their jobs.

Few things could seem more remote to entrepreneurs. But being outnumbered by the corporate working world, they may talk about getting rich and retiring. And if successful, entrepreneurs sometimes live out this corporate-world fantasy for about six months or a year. Then they come roaring back from Vermont or Europe for the excitement and personal fulfillment of making something happen again.

Entrepreneurs work long hours and thrive on the difficulty of the job. They seem truly happy when struggling against long odds and adverse circumstances. Executives satisfy these human needs through developing complicated hobbies and imaginative vacations. For the entrepreneur, the business serves as the hobby, vacation, and creative force.

Institutional investors and bankers generally distrust new venture people because they sense their differing motivations. They will not be simply jealous or envious of your attitudes and achievements, though this may be a factor in their feelings. More significantly, they will fear you do not care enough for profit and money, the denominations they understand best. And basically they will be right, you probably will not.

Bankers and institutional investors hoard money during prosperity and lament its loss during bad periods. Entrepreneurs usually react in just the opposite manner: they feel most challenged, exhilarated, and fulfilled during bleak times. They tend to feel nervous, unfulfilled, and unneeded during prosperity.

To improve your chances for success in founding your own business you must come to terms with these entrepreneurial values and their differences from those of the corporate world. Arthur Miller described a key entrepreneurial trait through the words of Willy Loman in *Death of a Salesman*: "A salesman [entrepreneur] is got to dream, boy. It comes with the territory." Indeed it does; when Willy stopped dreaming, he failed and died.

The true joy and reward of entrepreneurial life are the freedom and exhilaration of the new venture dream. To understand this phenomenon more clearly, listen to Edwin Land describe his cameras at the flamboyant Polaroid annual meetings or read about Henry Ford, Sr., glorifying his automobiles. I shared these emotions when passing an Umbroller stroller on the street. I used to lead my companions in a cheer when going by a retailer carrying one of our products. And when I saw a unit needing repair, I often fixed it on the spot.

Admittedly this enthusiasm can be a bit trying for your family and friends. While driving by F.A.O. Schwarz on a Christmas shopping trip in New York, I spotted a man struggling to open one of the special Umbrollers made for this famous toy store. In an impassioned moment, I rolled down the car window and bellowed the opening instructions to him. He heard me despite the traffic, crowds, and distance. He had a stunned look, for even in New York this was rather bizarre behavior. But I was not sufficiently cowed by the general reaction, so I shouted out the instructions again to the ire of honking cars behind me and the amusement of the Christmas crowd in general. For fear that I would leap out and bolt across the street, he opened the stroller on cue.

What convinced me of the normality of the situation was the nonchalance of my wife during the episode. Only later did I realize how many entrepreneurial spouses must have endured this kind of ritual. Henry Ford, Sr.'s commitment to his product was so strong he reputedly gave his son a new Ford for his sixteenth birthday—in pieces, ready for his son's assembly. Enthusiasm, dreams, and product commitment are what make both the small and great entrepreneurs tick.

Entrepreneurship may be your true vocation if Jefferson's aspirations and Willy Loman's dreams are important to you. On the other hand, if you view yourself as an impartial, tough-minded, money-motivated, bottom-line-oriented manager, you probably will not receive the pleasures from new venture life to sustain you through its bleakest hours.

Those talents are perfect for the corporate world. The hard-nosed, tough-guy approach requires an inplace organization to dominate and control; the new venture leader, on the other hand, must build an organization or system through gaining people's respect, commitment, and devotion. If entrepreneurs ever attempted the corporate style of domination, their first employees would abandon them long before the venture got off the ground.

If you think this idea is wrong, consider the character of successful entrepreneurs. Very few could be called tough-minded or bottom-line oriented. Most are somewhat impractical, partially cantankerous, and quite opinionated; but they are also born persuaders, committed dreamers, and fervent believers in their own products.

The strictly economic arguments for not pursuing an entrepreneurial career are quite simple; as in horse racing, the fastest way to lose your fortune is betting on the long shots. The high mortality rate for new enterprises is staggering. Four out of five fold within three years. Most of the survivors are just that, survivors, not prosperous businesses.

Major corporations can withstand numerous problems, a small company can barely survive one. In the small-company-dominated juvenile furniture industry, for example, 50 percent of the firms disappeared during the 1970s. Some went bankrupt, others dissolved, and the rest merged with larger corporations. Many of the former owners moved on to more lucrative jobs as employees in larger organizations.

Corporate life offers a predictably higher salary, better fringe benefits, and more job security. If it is simply money you desire, the commodity exchanges or stock markets are better risks than gambling on your bread-and-butter earnings. Simply put, the odds are overwhelmingly against your creating a new venture success.

Yet few opportunities exist in modern life to amass substantial wealth other than through founding your own company. As an entrepreneur, you need no longer wait for a public offering or create a long earnings history; big firms are seeking rapid expansion through the acquisition of small and large companies alike. As the pool of available companies has diminished, the major acquirers have sought out smaller enterprises more aggressively.

Today, selling out to the multinationals seems the most practical method of cashing in your investment, because indifference of underwriters and investors has made new stock issues increasingly difficult to sell. The irony of this is that you may have to sell your venture to the very organizations that, because of personal and career desires, you wanted to avoid. Many entrepreneurs resolve this dilemma by not selling out until they are prepared to move on to other projects.

The rewards of entrepreneurship are fragile and uncertain at best. For most entrepreneurs the process is its own reward. The financial benefits are of secondary importance to them. In reviewing your career goals, consider whether your needs match this profile. If not, you may do well to select another career.

WHY AVOID ENTREPRENEURSHIP

Since World War II, the risks associated with entrepreneurship have accelerated. The multinationals have contributed significantly to this shift by offering employees substantially higher and more secure compensation; job changing has lost most of its negative connotations, so executives do not fear firings, layoffs, mergers, and liquidations as much as they did years ago. The result of these changes has been that an increasing number of executives have become rich without ever having undergone the risks and hardships of running a new enterprise.

A second factor has been the growing restrictiveness of modern business life, which has affected small companies most severely. Government regulations have grown in most industries, creating mountains of paperwork and substantially increasing the overhead burden for most small firms.

These environmental changes have contributed to big-business growth because small companies can hardly afford the high overhead costs required to cope with the mushrooming complexities of business life. The regulators and their supporters may well be fair-minded people; indeed, many are small-business advocates as well. Yet they undermine their small-business convictions through pursuing regulatory actions which drain the time and resources of new ventures.

This increasingly restrictive business environment has forced even stable independent companies to seek shelter by associating themselves with members of the Fortune 500, who have the cash and clout to handle the growing intricacies and associated costs. The fast-food industry provides an excellent example. This market has witnessed a rapid consolidation period after years of small company prosperity. Burger King, Magic Pan, and Steak 'n Ale have all sought cover through acquisition by Pillsbury. Horn and Hardart, the famous New York restaurant chain, gave up their cafeterias, relinquished their independence, and restored their profits by becoming the exclusive New York City Burger King franchisee. Most markets have experienced similar consolidation as smaller companies quietly disappeared into the protective anonymity of the Fortune 500. As a result, the risks of starting a new company have greatly increased, since their potential competitors are progressively better financed and better able to blunt competitive inroads.

This, then, is the hazardous environment in which you must select your opportunity. New ventures traditionally prosper most in unregulated periods, such as late nineteenth-century America or postwar Europe. Clearly this is not the state of affairs today. Exercise special care to reduce the odds of becoming a new venture casualty yourself.

THE ENTREPRENEURIAL PROFILE

The choice of an entrepreneurial career is risky because new venture life is far easier begun than ended. Having the reputation of a maverick makes the transition back to corporate life difficult. People in large organizations have decidedly mixed feelings about the adventurous entrepreneurial type. While they may envy the bold, action-oriented approach, they fear the fast, instinctive decision-making style. Moreover, the entrepreneur usually finds it difficult to leave the exhilarating atmosphere of a new company for what he or she sees as the dull corporate world.

The irrevocable nature of the entrepreneurial career choice makes it essential that you weigh your decision carefully before leaping into the profession. Your first step should be to analyze your personal qualifications. Entrepreneurship is not one of the conventional professions that relies on intelligence, good training, and experience. The necessary talents are more similar to artistic or athletic skills that are dependent on native talents and abilities, though capable of improvement through training and practice.

The traits necessary for a successful new venture career can be illustrated effectively by comparing executive and entrepreneurial temperaments. The professional executive is like an iceberg that would melt in the hot chaotic climate of a new venture. The entrepreneur is similar to a tropical flower that would not survive in a cool, professional corporate environment. You must select a career suited to your particular temperament. Use this chapter to determine whether your personal resources are more appropriate for the professional-executive or creative-entrepreneur career. Perhaps you will judge yourself ill-suited to both and decide to look elsewhere still.

Many able entrepreneurs have gained valuable experience in the corporate world. But few ever achieved much professional distinction as executives. Some were alienated corporate lifers going nowhere. Others were young people trying out the corporate world before moving on to entrepreneurial careers. Virtually none were accomplished executives leaving their cozy corporate nests to embark on their own adventure. The successful transition from entrepreneur to executive is equally rare. Most entrepreneurs cannot make the transition to being a manager in their own companies once they are going concerns, let alone transfer back to the corporate environment in an alien company.

The traditional inability of executives and entrepreneurs to change careers indicates the substantial differences between the two pursuits. Your chance for new venture success is limited if you have mastered the corporate world. The reverse is equally true. You must make a career choice and focus your energies accordingly. An attempt to succeed in both will virtually guarantee failure in either career.

Executives must develop thorough management skills and detached dispositions to solve complex problems and preserve the existing assets of their corporations. Sales and profit growth must be subordinated to the defensive objectives of maintaining and preserving the corporate empire. If properly protected, the enormous multinational resources will inevitably grind out sufficient cash flow, sales growth, and profit to sustain themselves quite nicely. Earnings per share and growth goals become quite secondary and are emphasized mainly to impress the financial community. They are not particularly important to the individual executive's career.

The modern executive must resolve a complex assortment of problems. The task involves controlling vast amounts of cash, people, and assets. Many corporate empires sprawl vulnerably over several continents, adding more variables and problems to the executive's decision making.

The executive task is essentially custodial. Once the huge empire has been created, it must be protected and preserved by the curator-executive. The profession demands caution, experience, and technical expertise. The multinational corporation is like the *Queen Elizabeth 2*, so large and complex that its course can be changed only through slow, deliberate, planned, and cooperative effort. The ship would capsize if the executive foolishly employed the direct, immediate approach of the entrepreneur.

This custodial task tends to be performed best by conservative, cool, measured people who prefer an anonymous role. The best of these individuals come from the graduate business school programs that emphasize logic, analysis, caution, calmness, and risk aversion. Their career objectives focus on salary, security, position, and power considerations.

Entrepreneurs, on the other hand, must solve basic problems and create corporate assets. Sales and profit growth are essential for new venture survival. Earnings per share and positive cash flow goals must be the predominant new enterprise objectives. Without emphasizing these goals, the new company would stand only a remote chance of survival.

The entrepreneur must resolve concrete problems such as meeting payrolls, selling customers, hiring and firing employees, and pacifying creditors. At first the company will be the entrepreneur alone; he or she must have the temperament and skills to master these problems alone. Little cash, few assets, and no stability exist to assist them in their task or protect the volatile venture from oblivion. The business is agonizingly simple, though not at all easy, and the problems all too obvious and pressing.

The entrepreneurial role is therefore highly individualistic and creative. The company must be erected where nothing existed before. The job demands enthusiasm, endurance, conclusiveness, leadership, pride in one's product, marketing skills, nerve, and shrewdness. The new enterprise is like a dinghy; one wave could sink the entire vessel. Changing courses is frequently required to permit survival. The dinghy would sink if the entrepreneur foolishly waited for a measured, long-term analysis of what to do. When the waves rise up, no time is ever available for deliberation; the entrepreneur must act immediately or risk oblivion. Above all, he or she must have the talent to react quickly.

The creative entrepreneurial task is best executed by people with a shrewd, bold, and instinctive nature. This makes for a rare combination of traits, since shrewd minds often lack the more irrational, less cautious capacity to act. The true entrepreneur has a decisive nature and loves to act on instinct. These rather bold types are generally loners who can relate well to people when they so choose. Their career goals emphasize achievement, excitement, independence, and personal job satisfaction. Money, position, and status count principally as measurements of their success rather than as ends in themselves. They take little pride in them except when tormenting former critics and adversaries.

Compare for a moment the contrasting temperaments and skills demanded by the entrepreneurial and executive careers. One can hardly imagine more divergent personality profiles. And few successful executives or entrepreneurs seem to vary much from these portraits; so make sure you select the field most congenial to your personality or you will suffer untold agonies trying to adopt a foreign identity. For the purposes of your self-analysis, the following pages describe the key entrepreneurial traits in more depth.

Enthusiasm and Endurance

Irrepressible enthusiasm and the endurance to withstand setbacks seem to be crucial entrepreneurial trademarks. The true entrepreneurial response upon learning that the only factory has burned down is, "Well, we didn't need that plant anyway!" These traits must bolster the new venture through the impossible troubles that stalk it. Few companies would have reached the going-concern stage without the inflated confidence of their founders. Entrepreneurs tend to be like eighteen-year-old marines who believe the bullets will go right through them without hurt or harm; without this bravado they probably could not endure what awaits them.

This powerful conviction radiates confidence to employees, suppliers, lenders, and customers, who often remain loyal and supportive despite overwhelming reasons to desert the enterprise. Late payrolls, overdue debts, and delayed shipments cause many arguments that are soon forgotten as in a lovers' quarrel. The entrepreneurial enthusiasm and endurance restores good feelings like a marvelous tonic.

Professional executive training and experience totally undermine this crucial talent. Corporate experience carefully dismantles dreamers and turns them into cautious curators, quick to sound the alarm over any possible pitfall. The executive analyzes the total risks involved in long-term business projects; the entrepreneur just worries about capturing the next account. Instinctively, entrepreneurs seem to recognize that considering all the risks involved in a new business would paralyze them and prevent them from taking necessary action.

Failure, frustration, anxiety, and defeat form the new company diet. The enterprise is continually let down by employees, suppliers, customers, and lenders. The entrepreneur must have the enthusiasm and endurance to survive the pain and maintain vitality. It is not a career for the weakhearted and precise. Those types would be swallowed up in the agony and overwhelmed by the chaos. New venture success results from how many punches you can take, not from how many you can give.

The first task of a new enterprise illustrates this personal requirement quite vividly. A stable economic entity must be created where nothing stood before. To imagine this more precisely, walk into a business office and visualize it empty of people, furniture, and records. The entrepreneur must develop all of it. He or she must find competent people to work for the unstable, unknown firm; purchase office equipment with no money; develop a recordkeeping system from scratch; persuade suppliers and customers to rely on an unfamiliar entity; and fund the entire operation with little or no cash.

Entrepreneurs must slug their way through each of these obstacles, recover from the inevitable setbacks, and forge on. Every entrepreneur remembers these agonies all too clearly. In my first venture, it took three hires (two fires), four months, and endless hours of training before I developed my first adequate secretary. Two months later she moved out of town and I had to start all over again. It took several negotiating sessions before convincing an office supplier to ship supplies to our new company; only after all the financial arrangements had been approved did I discover his products were inadequate for our specialized needs. Back to square one again. These small, irritating problems are the daily fare of a new venture.

Few outsiders have any conception of these entrepreneurial agonies. Executives take for granted their corporate structure and its status in the business world. Suppliers, customers, lenders, and employees desire to be associated with them. Each may haggle over terms and conditions, but they will generally be delighted to deal with the established corporation on some basis. Most of them, however, will not deal with a new venture on any terms.

"Who the hell are you?" is the unstated question that plagues the new enterprise and its managers. The dilemma requires an individual combining marathoner endurance and evangelical zeal to persuade people to deal with his or her dream. Only then can the entrepreneur begin to execute the traditional business tasks of marketing, sales, finance, and operations.

Conclusiveness

Conclusive decision-making is imperative, since a new venture must move to survive. To wait or linger is to court extinction. The new company has too many things to accomplish, in spite of its having an inadequate organization, limited assets, and no laurels to rest on. The entrepreneur must drive the company forward despite weariness, second guessing, and recriminations. The waters will be uncharted and the issues unclear; yet this problem only underscores the need for a decisive person willing to make conclusive decisions in an atmosphere of uncertainty.

The fledgling company has no sales, production, or financial history to fall back on. Little research is available because of its short history and underfinancing. Records are inadequate because systems and people are new. Little time or money exists to upgrade either. Yet, even though conditions are so unsettled, the new venture must have the best possible operating plan. This makes the new venture a candidate for the familiar airlines joke: "I have one piece of good news for you, and one of bad. We are traveling at record speed, but we are lost!"

It is this uncertain environment that places such a premium on conclusive decisions. The new venture may become extinct if it waits for the best information. The entrepreneur must act on limited facts and revise or reverse directions later, when better information becomes available. You cannot avoid a decision by not acting; no action is in itself a decision. Do not fall prey to the frequent executive delusion that decisions can be postponed without paying substantial penalties.

The entrepreneur must keep the decision-making process fluid by making decisions promptly. New ventures must make more decisions than established corporations because every issue must be decided for the first time, from selecting employees to choosing a bookkeeping system. Established companies know their targets;

your company must continually select new targets as your marketing team learns more about your product and its natural marketplace. Established firms can draw upon proven employees from within the company; entrepreneurs must hire employees from the outside because no inside personnel pool exists. The need for conclusiveness in the face of the multitude of new situations extends to dealing with financial services, outside contractors, professional services, and other assorted problems. Without a decisive nature, the founder will fold under the relentless pressure to act.

No matter how small the issue, even the most decisive entrepreneur is prone to believe that each decision may destroy the entire venture. You must have the fiber to resist these fears and plunge forward so the next decisions can be attended to and resolved. Delay of the decision process will clog the system and create an unhealthy, constipated condition. If you are not temperamentally conclusive, spare yourself the suffering and select another career.

Leadership

I have yet to meet a successful entrepreneur who was not a natural leader. Some are whimsical and cantankerous; others are quiet and technical. But at the opportune moment, they can emerge from these moods to lead their company out of harm's way. They are often like the Pied Piper, turning around to find a group following them wherever they go. They can ignite their followers almost at will. They have the remarkable talent of being able to inspire devotion and loyalty, mustering excellent performances from average people. This is an indispensable entrepreneurial talent.

Do not be deceived by their seemingly disarming and indirect approaches such as "I am just an engineer," or "I don't know, what do you think?" They avoid the autocratic presence of many executives to put you at your ease and gain your confidence. They make their own ideas seem as if they were yours all along. Like the great performers they so often are, entrepreneurs have superb timing and rarely miss a cue. After all, who convinced those Wall Street hard-boiled eggs that another Edison was creating photographic gold at Polaroid. Just some blue-sky inventor from Cambridge, Massachusetts!

Product Pride

Few characteristics distinguish the executive from the entrepreneur more clearly than product pride. Executives will use competitive products with few qualms, even with a wily detached glee on occasion, while most entrepreneurs would rather die first. The executive world promotes a cool, detached posture; to fall in love with your own products is to sacrifice dignity, objectivity, and judgment. The entrepreneur believes in a totally involved attitude; not to love your product is to settle for mediocrity, complacency, and boredom.

These attitudes are solidly based in rational self-interest. A General Motors executive refusing to rent a Hertz Ford would be wasting energy on a gallant gesture. The complicated problems confronting him or her as an executive do not permit time for futile encounters with Hertz clerks. The potential argument would also appear undignified and, perhaps, a little silly, since he or she may be working for Ford someday. So, with a slightly ironic smile, the executive usually lets the incident pass.

Entrepreneurs, however, cannot afford to compromise product convictions because they know that they alone set and maintain the rigorous product quality and loyalty code in their companies. It is this pride in one's product that is so often the equalizer for small companies in competition with major corporations. Customers, suppliers, creditors, and employees feel the vigilant attention given to product standards, company performance, and themselves. And this, above all else, is what undoubtedly influences them to work with the new venture.

At Cross River the office workers worked harder, for less money, and under worse conditions than in most comparable Westchester offices. Yet we had superb morale; the product commitment, excitement, and resulting *esprit de corps* made everyone feel useful and important. This commitment must start with you. Everyone else is simply part of the supporting cast. They will take their lead from your example. Product conviction is an important new venture advantage; protect it carefully.

Marketing Skills

Entrepreneurs with a marketing background usually have the best chance for success, since marketing and sales are the crucial functions in a new venture. Marketing entrepreneurs often require financial or operations people, but, even alone, they stand the best shot at success.

Marketing entrepreneurs may disguise themselves as engineers, line managers, inventors, or financial wizards. And, indeed, they may have these other skills as well. Yet underneath the surface rests a consummate salesperson or marketing genius. Edwin Land of Polaroid is a perfect example of the disguised marketing talent.

He has inspired both the photographic and financial world with his products, ideas, and presentations. His company has an aura of product integrity few firms can match. High quality, important purpose, and financial growth have become almost synonymous with the Polaroid name despite numerous setbacks in the actual marketplace. Land may be an engineering genius, but I suspect his greatest contribution has been his marketing vision and selling know-how.

Remember that the finest marketing and sales entrepreneurs often disclaim the title, as Land so often does, to disarm the outside world. Do not be misled by this ploy in assessing your own abilities and judging your career options. If you are not marketing oriented, be absolutely sure to have a marketing partner on your team from the beginning—or do not go into business for yourself.

Nerve and Shrewdness

Entrepreneurs must have the nerve and shrewdness to put the whole company together and keep it alive. They must make lemonade out of lemons; they compete with water pistols while their competitors have cannons. Only the shrewd, bold ones can avoid being cornered, panicked, and obliterated.

Your principal new venture task will be to persuade people, companies, suppliers, and customers to do business with your shaky new enterprise. Each outsider must be sized up carefully. Nerve and shrewdness will be your primary tools in dealing with them.

At our first Cross River trade show, Alex Goodwin and I desperately needed company and product recognition. We sacrificed dignity and decorum to achieve this. Friends masqueraded as users of our new stroller and we buttonholed buyers in bars, coffee shops, rest rooms, hotel lobbies, and other likely spots. The effect was brash, unprofessional, and somewhat rude. That was the price for establishing our product and corporate identity promptly, and getting some desperately needed purchase orders as a result. We found it better to be thought of badly than not at all.

Our first communications were geared to solve the same problem. Cross River was presented as an aggressive, substantial, active company worth doing business with. Many conservative critics, customers, and competitors questioned the tastefulness of our approach. But, as the J.C. Penney buyer told me wryly, "Do not be apologetic about your supposedly inappropriate behavior. I am always interested in companies that are so ruthlessly maligned by their competitors. They must be doing something right to worry them so much!" Our aggressiveness soon catapulted us into the industry eye and eventually led to our becoming a venerable member of the industry establishment.

A new venture is continually under the gun and dealing from a position of weakness: little cash, too few customers, low credit lines, untrained employees, inexperienced operations management, and too much change. Your nerve and shrewdness must galvanize these vulnerable areas into a stable enterprise. You must, in other words, make your assets work twenty times harder for your firm than the same ones would for an executive's corporation—or your venture will surely fail.

HOW DO YOU MEASURE UP?

The new enterprise equalizers are the intangible talents of the entrepreneur: enthusiasm, endurance, conclusiveness, leadership, product pride, marketing skills, nerve, and shrewdness. Without a strong dose of these qualities, your venture will flounder like a wounded duck. These traits will have more influence on your success than the best business plans, product and market selections, or financing packages. With the appropriate personal resources, you should make one of your enterprises succeed. Without these characteristics, you can fail in a virtually ideal opportunity, as so many entrepreneurs have.

You must judge your personality carefully before choosing either an entrepreneurial or executive career. The insights of close friends and associates can be helpful and may even surprise you. If you are aware of personal shortcomings, you may be able to adjust your personality traits somewhat to fit the career requirements. Be careful, though, to assess whether the change is worth the personal cost. The new venture joy will not be there to bolster you through hard times unless you have a personality conducive to the task. It is far better to make an honest judgment in the beginning, decline the opportunity, and avoid the potential personal, financial, and career risks. So before going further, consider carefully whether you really want to ride the entrepreneurial whirlwind. Once begun, it is hard to get off.

Formation

MARKET SELECTION

The first step in forming a company is choosing a suitable market. Avoiding the wrong market is far more important for new venture survival than selecting the right one. One unforeseen rock can sink your fragile vessel. This need for caution is one reason why so many successful entrepreneurs are bedrock conservatives by disposition. They may have missed innumerable chances to be even more successful, but they have carefully avoided high-risk projects. In selecting a market, this cautious avoidance should be stressed over aggressive action. Your limited cash and credit resources should be the principal restraining factors in your market evaluation. To improve your odds for corporate survival, you must emphasize these constraints when selecting a market.

A positive cash flow should be emphasized over growth and profit opportunities, since new ventures fail because of a lack of cash, not an absence of profit. Growth is usually absorbed successfully by firms with positive cash flows; however, growth usually strangles new ventures with negative cash flows. All new venture hopes and aspirations disintegrate without sufficient cash to meet payrolls and pay creditors. Cautious market selection can go a long way toward avoiding negative cash-flow problems, since the conditions of each market often dictate cash expenditure and cash collection practices.

The principal markets to avoid are those that are capital intensive, have a short product life cycle, extend credit too easily, and are large in size. All require cash and credit commitments beyond the capacity of most startup ventures. The Fortune 500 dominate most of these markets by using their huge capital resources to fence out small-company intrusions. Remember that sufficient capital is one ingredient your company will surely not have. Do not compete with large companies, if at all possible; large firms can afford short-term negative cash flows to build strong businesses that earn positive cash flows at a later date. Your adventure could not survive the waiting period.

Capital Intensive Markets

The capital intensive benchmark is the dollar sales to dollar investment ratio. The appropriate market should have at least a ten-to-one ratio to maximize the return on your limited capital and improve your prospects for survival. This means that $500,000 in annual sales should be generated by no more than $50,000 of capital.

The soft-goods business represents such a market opportunity. One investment dollar can generate over twenty sales dollars. The result is an entrepreneurial haven with numerous new entries each year. Bad years witness many bankruptcies, since the companies' capital positions are often heavily leveraged; but the ease of market entry permits former entrepreneurs to get back into the business relatively simply. This is the type of market you should select to increase your odds for survival.

The beer industry is a classic example of a market to avoid, since it is effectively fenced off by the Fortune 500. Each sales dollar requires at least one invested capital dollar. As a result, the national giants such as Budweiser and Miller have squeezed out the smaller, financially weaker regional firms. Forced mergers, liquidations, and bankruptcies have been the order of business as competitors have been reduced by over 60 percent in the last decade alone, with more consolidation occurring each year.

Short Product Life-Cycle Markets

It costs a great deal of money to bring new products to market. Short product life-cycle markets require repeated capital investments to introduce new products in order to keep up with current market trends and insure survival. These markets demand unusual corporate stability to withstand the inevitable bad products, poor introductions, and costly disruptions caused by failures. Ford could survive the Edsel quite nicely; your unstable, undercapitalized firm could not.

Various packaged-goods markets exemplify this phenomenon. Enormous amounts of speculative capital are devoted exclusively to new-product development, testing, and introduction. The aggressive financial commitment has driven many small companies to liquidate or merge with larger firms to acquire the capital muscle to compete and survive in these rapidly emerging marketplaces.

The Procter & Gambles, General Foods, and General Mills have increased their new product introductions to improve market share, outdistance their smaller competitors, and force acquisitions. The coffee market offers a perfect example. The brands have proliferated; yet the number of producing companies has gradually declined. Maxwell House, Max Pak, ADC, Yuban, Brim, International Coffees, and Mellow Roast all come from just one company—General Foods. The major companies keep the competition intramural by introducing new products to outflank smaller companies' old, staple products.

These markets are ripe for entrepreneurial innovation, but the accelerated pace of new product introductions makes entering them less than attractive for new ventures. Even one poor new-product introduction will usually sink a stable new venture. Beware of rapidly evolving markets—your enterprise may not have the financial strength to chase the evolution.

Easy Credit-Term Markets

Many industries thrive on liberal credit-term policies to encourage customer orders. This phenomenon is harder to identify than the other negative market factors because it is generally not well publicized by either customers or suppliers. The first indication of it in an industry is the practice of granting credit to

virtually any firm and extending terms to good risks. The office
equipment, retail, and toy industries employ this tactic with
abandon. The market leaders in these fields use their capital
leverage over smaller firms to expand their market shares aggressively by implementing liberal credit policies.

The second approach is leasing, by which companies provide
their customers with a substantial asset but require only small
monthly payments in return. This practice expands product sales,
although it places pressure on their working-capital levels. As
a result, it effectively fences smaller companies out of markets by
requiring that they have a substantial capital base to underwrite a
leasing program.

It should be of little surprise, then, that the escalation of
liberal credit policies in the toy market encouraged substantial
industry consolidation. Fisher-Price and Leo Marx were both
acquired by Quaker Oats; Creative Playthings was purchased by
CBS. The resulting capital infusions permitted each acquired
company to increase its market share and profits through relying on
its parent's financial strength to offer better terms. As a new
venture, you must remain alert to changes in industry credit
policies because these transformations can occur as quickly as
a flash flood. If they touch your market, seek cover quickly. A
factor or leasing company may offer temporary relief; the continued use of liberal credit, though, will lead to substantial industry liquidations, mergers, and acquisitions. Be vigilant about
these marketplace changes.

Large Markets

Large markets should be avoided because each percentage of
market share is too valuable for the competition to ignore and
economy of scale gives your competitors a tremendous cost-
efficiency edge. Your marketing inroads will only bring strong
competitive response. New companies need leadtime to build a
solid sales and operations base before encountering direct competition. This is virtually impossible in most large markets, where
product monitoring and research is a refined art.

In a small market, competitors must worry about their own survival before considering the competition. By the time your firm has become a legitimate threat, your business may have achieved a size comparable to your competitors'. In the juvenile furniture market, Cross River reached five million dollars annual sales before encountering substantial competitive response. Since the largest firm in the industry was approximately twelve million dollars at the time, we had enough relative size to weather the competitive storm and survive quite nicely by capitalizing on our product leadtime, expertise in our product segment, and our retail distribution. However, if our major competitor had had sales of eighty million dollars, we may well have been driven out of business.

The economy of scale advantage of a large corporation is almost insurmountable for a new venture. Large companies can defray overhead and operating costs over large unit volumes, while your firm must absorb similar costs over smaller quantities. These competitors can afford expensive cost-reduction projects based on their high volumes. In most instances, such opportunities would make no sense for your firm, with its lower volume levels; your product would become more and more uncompetitive, on a cost basis, in the marketplace. Smaller markets, no matter how entrenched your competition, do not offer similar advantages to the other firms.

Small companies survive and prosper in very few large markets. One is hard-pressed to think of any, in fact. Autos, energy, metals, appliances, glass, and other major industries are usually composed of and dominated by a few large producers. Even Chrysler is considered a "small" automotive firm. Their vulnerability stems from having competitors four and five times their size; even eight billion dollars in sales does not put them on an equal footing with their competition.

Rapidly expanding small markets often hold similar dangers for new ventures. Once the overall market achieves a certain size, the major corporations move in and take control. The calculator market is such an example. The small firms dominated in the developmental stages; then their Fortune 500 suppliers—Rockwell International and Texas Instruments—became interested, and within a few years they dominated the industry.

The small calculator firms needed positive cash flows for survival; the major companies were willing to endure short-term negative cash flows to expand production, reduce costs, and insure future profits. This rapid marketplace change underscores the need for entrepreneurial foresight and vigilance. Yesterday's dream market may be tomorrow's graveyard.

What Markets to Select

Since mainstream, growth-oriented markets should be excluded, this leaves you small stable markets to pursue. These markets have less appeal for major companies because the total profit potential is limited. Numerous major corporations looked to the $200 million juvenile furniture market for acquisitions; this was particularly true of toy companies, since they were in a closely related industry. Yet the low potential payout discouraged the multibillion-dollar companies such as Quaker Oats and General Mills. A few $100 million conglomerates plunged in, but the low profit potential caused most of them to divest themselves of their purchases.

So concentrate on what markets to avoid. Then, if at all possible, choose a market you are familiar with. Contrary to much talk about the perfect market or product idea, I have found opportunities in almost every market I have considered. The trick is in the execution, not the idea.

Successful ventures are built on marketing opportunities. These opportunities usually occur in market niches where the leaders have rested on the laurels of their past performance. The industry leaders may have forgotten that product leadership is a transitory and impermanent phenomenon.

Your product innovation need not be spectacular to succeed. Indeed, it may go unnoticed and uncopied for longer if it is not too original. It must capitalize on a need recognized by your potential customers. The best products are often recombinations of known elements that make the product right for today's customer.

At Cross River we capitalized on our competitors' convictions that strength, not convenience, was the critical factor to the stroller purchaser. The stickfolding Umbroller stroller combined known stroller elements but functioned more conveniently than previous models. Competitors ignored the product because of their biases, and this gave our company critical leadtime in the marketplace. Retailers saw the marketplace need and gave the company distribution. By the time the competition responded, Cross River was an established stroller manufacturer with a 20 percent share of the market. While the competition copied our old success, we moved on to the next product generation.

This type of marketing opportunity seems to exist in every small market: Enough good markets exist that you do not need to gamble your future on an unknown or high-risk market. Once you have chosen a market, the question of having a partner or partners should be your next concern.

PARTNERS: THE NEW VENTURE TRAP

Conventional wisdom suggests your firm stands a better chance of survival with partners than without them. Partners supposedly provide balance by offering complementary strengths to bolster the areas of your weakness. This approach may work in a college environment where interaction and education are the principal objectives. However, in a new business, partnership often diverts management energies from direct action and submerges them in internal discussions, bickering, and conferences.

Since partners must be consulted on key issues, they necessarily slow down the decision-making process. The time lost through this counseling usually jeopardizes results rather than improves them. As a result, successful partnerships seem to be either alter ego relationships or relationships in which each partner never intrudes in the other's territory.

These situations are relatively rare. So the odds are against a smoothly functioning partnership without even considering the other handicaps to the relationship. I have had only one successful partnership, with Alex Goodwin and Jim Sloan at Cross River. Several others had promise but became ineffective or unsatisfactory for a variety of reasons. As a consequence, I now pursue my business activities without partners.

If you can manage alone, you should generally do so. If not, read on carefully. No trickier problem exists for most new enterprises than the correct selection of partners. New companies have probably failed more often because of this problem than any other.

These failures occur so frequently because partners must deal with each other under trying circumstances and on a daily basis. Small differences tend to become magnified. These disputes, in turn, divide the organization into factions. Then the partnership conflicts take on all of the negative associations of a family fight. The resulting emotional turmoil can be far more disruptive than the worst marketplace, financial, or production problems. All of this can paralyze a new company.

Because of the potential seriousness of this problem, your partners should be selected with all the care with which you would have liked to have chosen your family. The causes for poor selection usually are inexperienced judgment and a lack of foresight regarding the impact of corporate growth and change.

At the inception of the company, you will be most inexperienced at selecting, evaluating, and training people. Yet it is at this stage that you must make your most important selection—the corporate family. If the enterprise succeeds, it will pass through various stages of growth which will have a profound impact on your partners' job requirements, egos, self-concepts, and financial lives. Predicting the impact of these changes is a difficult matter. The most solid people and stable relationships tremble under the assault of such changes.

Ultimately, your choice of partners will be a very subjective one. Not many of us can look objectively at the individual who worked long hours on prototypes in the cellar, pounded the pavement when no one knew or cared about the company, or invested his or her last dollar in our dream. Despite these emotional obstacles, you must be able to make the most realistic judgment about your potential partners, for everyone's sake.

Some common partnership traps are:

* I owe it to them.
* They worked hard in the beginning.
* It is owed to me.
* I worked hard in the beginning.
* (They) brought the product, invention, technology, money, or whatever to the venture.

These traps can be summarized in the two words: past orientation. Most prospective partners discuss their importance as if the firm were established, profitable, and listed on the New York Stock Exchange. In fact, most of the work is ahead of you at this stage; often, the first sale has not even been made. A sale does not mean all the people who "liked the idea," who would "give you a test," and who will "give you the order." There is no sale until you have the purchase order and have shipped the goods. When Ford introduced the Edsel their surveys demonstrated conclusively that people "liked the idea." They just never got around to buying the product.

Despite feelings related to "how hard everyone has worked," the initial spade work is of little long-term consequence. Partners must be compensated for their *future* contributions to the company. Yet, as in most family situations, the issues tend to settle into the past, into what was done rather than what will be accomplished. It is essential to be oriented to the future or your firm will be dangerously burdened with old obligations. It is one thing for Exxon or IBM to take past problems upon themselves voluntarily, for they have the resources to afford the luxury. Your firm does not.

At this stage your fledgling firm has no value to anyone other than yourselves. Consequently, you must be tough-minded in your evaluation of how your partner will benefit the enterprise in the future. If you cannot reach a meeting of the minds, you should clean house immediately. This may mean dumping the product or company. Even if this is the case, you are usually better off doing so. Your first loss is always your best one.

I had to make a particularly agonizing decision of this sort myself. The incident involved a superior product in the home shelving market that I hoped to use to launch my third venture. The company proceeded extraordinarily well in the initial stages. The prototypes were good, the contractor was solid, our financing was lined up, and the sales prospects were excellent. Then my partner began to act in what I believed to be an irrational manner.

Even though I knew him to be a fine individual, I nevertheless decided to follow my own advice and clean house by setting up two distinct companies, each of us owning one of them. The market was so enormous that we could both succeed without detracting from the other's progress. My suggestion was regarded as unacceptable; he wanted 100 percent ownership of the company, even though he was unwilling to compensate me for any investment. So I made an offer to buy him out. Although he was unwilling to pay me, he wanted $100,000 for his share. We had not debugged our first prototype, written our first purchase order, or received significant financing, but in his mind we were already New York Stock Exchange material.

The issue was never settled, the product never produced, and the company fizzled out. I later learned that this situation was not at all unusual; partnership squabbles are probably the major cause for new venture failures in the startup phase. If you find yourself in a similar situation, do not be embarrassed or afraid to bail out. As in poker, the secret to winning is knowing when to get out and minimize your losses.

Evaluation Process

General Motors can afford to carry unproductive people; your new company cannot. This may not be the way you would like things to be, but these are the economic realities of small-company life. The partnership evaluation is especially important for this reason: you simply cannot afford to carry an unproductive partner on the payroll over a long period of time.

The first principle in partnership evaluation should be that if it does not feel right, it is definitely wrong. If you feel at all nervous or ambivalent about your prospective partner, do not consider going into business with him or her no matter how attractive the situation may appear. Your emotional response, as a rule, will be far truer to reality than your intellectual reaction in these personal matters. You will *feel* problems before your intellect can articulate them. And above all, remember that if problems exist in the beginning, no matter how slight they may seem, they will explode under the inevitable pressures of a growing business.

If you still feel comfortable about your choice at this point, apply the banker's four Cs (character, capacity, capital, and credit rating) test to the individual and evaluate him or her against the entrepreneurial traits listed in Chapter 1. Character is the most important ingredient. The company will never succeed without a partner of character, despite the image the media project of successful entrepreneurs with no integrity. Many successful entrepreneurs have a limited moral perspective, but within their limitations they usually have a strong sense of honor and fair play.

Most entrepreneurs typecast themselves in the role of the tough guy. Their hard-boiled exterior is usually developed to withstand the daily onslaught of pressures and demands. When they feel betrayed, rage is an instant reaction, but in most cases they respond openly. Be on the lookout for the other type, the individual who is genuinely thick-skinned and unfeeling. These dangerous and usually unsuccessful types feel attracted to the image of entrepreneurship and can create disaster in any corporation. Beware of the real tough guy.

Capacity is the second most important trait. Your partner must have the intellectual and emotional capacity to grow with your business and its responsibilities, and not succumb to its pressures, rewards, and temptations. Study how your potential partner reacts to the four crucial tasks described in the first part of Chapter 3. Capacity, or the lack of it, is a trait that will run through his or her response to all of them.

A common business myth to beware of is that people desire more responsible jobs. By and large they do not. They may want the trappings of greater responsibility such as money, position, and power, but most of them do not want the responsibility itself. People interested in new venture careers are particularly susceptible to this flaw; they like the dream of an easy road to riches.

A related problem is the basement tinkerer, missionary salesperson, or inventor who may want to work hard but does not have the capacities to cope with the venture as it evolves into a two- or three-million-dollar business. Consider how the candidate will hold up under the scrutiny of a Sears buying committee or Citicorp loan officer, or under the harassment of a Teamsters official. It is a trying transition from prideful shirtsleeves to corporate management. Very few entrepreneurs make the change successfully; make sure your prospective partner at least has a good chance.

The banker's final two Cs, credit rating and capital, can be lumped together. A solid personal credit rating and financial status do not assure success. However, a shaky credit rating and financial status usually indicate potential failure.

A good or bad credit rating relates only secondarily to the amount of money someone earns. It has more to do with his or her willingness to meet obligations in a timely, responsible manner. According to Citicorp credit analysis, for instance, the best credit ratings are often earned by people with modest income and capital levels, who plan their financial lives within their salary and capital limits. An individual who follows this pattern will usually make a responsible business partner.

The worst credit ratings are often held by high earners who are flamboyant spenders. They may have high income and capital levels but still overspend. They do not reliably meet their commitments as a result. These people are often tempted to become entrepreneurs. No matter how much money your company can earn, they can outspend it.

The individual who has a good credit rating and capital to protect, even if it is just equity in a house and some savings, may not necessarily be right for the job—but at least he or she will be not wrong for it. This kind of person will probably apply similar economic principles to your business. A poor credit rating, on the other hand, means a high-risk partner. When your company needs cash, this individual will be flying first class and leasing a new Mercedes. The big spender will be delighted if you join in, but, of course, you will go down the drain that much faster.

The only truly reliable way of substantiating your analysis is to conduct a detailed investigation into the candidate's background. It will be one of the soundest investments you ever make. Keep the investigation aboveboard; in other words, you should let your potential partner know in advance that you are making these inquiries. In the process, cover the complete history, from education and work to credit and criminal records.

Many partnership problems could have been resolved at the outset if the principals openly evaluated each other. They would then not be compelled to lie or to cover up past sins. A clear understanding of past records prevents you from associating with undesirable people. The open evaluation sets a tone of candor which will be an invaluable standard for the new business.

The increased mobility of individuals in our society means we know less and less about the people we deal with. The traditional indications of success and failure have blended together and faded away. Changing jobs, homes, and families used to have clearly negative associations. This is no longer always the case; in fact, these changes are often thought to signify imagination and growth. The person who lives a stable and unvarying personal and professional life is often regarded as unpromising.

The haziness caused by these changing social values makes the partnership evaluation process even more complex and confusing to the new entrepreneur. I learned firsthand the importance of a personal investigation when I almost became involved with a seemingly presentable, competent man who turned out to have a substantial criminal record. Only through a routine personal inquiry did I uncover his unsavory background and avoid becoming entangled with him. The kinds of people interested in taking entrepreneurial risks are of an unusual type; be sure their differences are the right ones.

Investigation

A competent private investigator can provide you with a complete report for less than one thousand dollars if you provide enough specific biographical detail for the investigator to check up on. A detailed résumé should include full legal name, social security number, driver's license number, educational and work history with the appropriate dates, and addresses and phone numbers of personal and professional references. This should provide enough information for the investigator to check up on the individual relatively quickly and inexpensively. The private investigator should come recommended by your accountant, lawyer, or another professional. There are simply too many pitfalls associated with the unknown private investigator.

Goals of the Partners

Each partner should submit a sheet with his or her personal expectations noted in detail. This should include salary and fringe benefits, stock percentages, role within the company, long-range objectives, and possible changes in all of these as the company grows and prospers. You will be amazed at what you may read. Many disputes could be resolved in the beginning if partners reviewed their written goals with each other and used these documents as a basis to settle partnership problems as they arose.

This process uncovered several potential conflicts between potential partners and myself. In one instance, a minority partner wanted a second stock grant if the venture succeeded—to come from me, of course. His rationale was that if the company prospered, my smaller share would be enough for me. Another minority stockholder wanted to become chief executive if the enterprise succeeded, although I was ratified as the CEO (chief executive officer) from the beginning. His logic was that I would get the company to succeed and that would be my reward; then, he should have the pleasure of holding the title afterward. A partnership goal document worked in both instances to settle these potential difficulties before they occurred. In one case, I decided not to participate in the venture; in the other, we worked out a compromise suitable to us both.

Who Is the Boss?

Committees accomplish little except reports. Committees of two qualify for the same indictment. You must clearly designate a CEO from the beginning and stick by your choice. The CEO must be empowered to rule on every issue relating to the management of the company. He or she should be backed up by stock and board-of-director approval as the undisputed CEO or should have a written employment contract explicitly granting full CEO powers. This is often the first tough decision between partners. If you cannot decide it equitably, do not go into business together.

Partners rarely find the CEO selection an easy matter. Yet outsiders generally size up the situation rather simply and feel the choice is obvious. To make the best decision, consider it from the point of view of an unbiased outsider.

The only issue should be who is best suited to develop the resources of your new venture and take it to the going-concern stage. It does not matter who brought the most to the company in terms of money, product ideas, experience, or the like. Despite this, the major investor generally becomes the CEO, even though the size of a partner's investment is often a poor criterion. If you believe the choice is wrong, resign from the business; a new venture has virtually no chance for survival if the selected CEO is wrong for the job.

The appropriate grounds for selecting the right individual

should include business education, work experience, and the ability to work well with people. It is understood that the partner has genuine entrepreneurial traits and has passed the banker's four Cs test, or you would not have progressed to this stage. In addition, the potential CEO should have solid grounding in either cash or sales management, since these will be the first tough areas for the new firm. Operations and technology people usually make poor choices, since their interests diverge widely from cash and sales concerns. Professionals (lawyers, accountants, consultants) make poor selections because they earn their livelihoods by recommending, not by doing.

Quite frequently the reverse logic applies for Fortune 500 companies. Since these companies have developed far-flung organizations and huge asset bases, professionals and operations people are often perfect CEO choices because they are conservative, measured, and cautious recommenders. These people often make perfect executive-curators. However, your little company must make its mark; you need a creative pioneer in charge.

CORPORATE NAME

Since the principal corporate objective is the creation of a stable economic entity, your corporate name should suggest conservatism and financial stability. The name should suggest the nineteenth century, not the twenty-first. It should be simple, spellable, memorable, have dignity, and not be catchy or faddish.

Consider the straightforward names of the best-known growth companies: Avon, Data General, Digital Equipment, Eastman Kodak, IBM, and K Mart. Many of the blue chips have even more solid-sounding names: the Generals—Foods, Mills, and Motors; the Founders—Ford, Procter & Gamble, and Sears.

An early name for Cross River, I am embarrassed to admit, was "Best-in-the-World," an exaggeration, to put it mildly. When we saw that this name had a way of inspiring either annoyance or laughter, we tried to hide its pomposity under the flashy variation of "BIW Group," telling people the initials stood for "Brown" (me) and "Ingersoll and Wilson," silent partners if there ever were any, since they did not exist. Jim Sloan (a Cross River partner and operations manager) kept sending us prototypes, however, under an even earlier name, Brown Brothers Wilson. Finally I asked him why and he said, "When I use Brown Brothers Wilson they give me instant credit and treat my package with respect. When I use BIW Group, they snicker and ask me for cash on the barrelhead." A name hunt started at that moment.

Cross River was selected because it evoked the image of stability, simplicity, and longevity. It passed the air freight test of gaining credit and inspiring respect. All stationery and communications used subdued lettering and designs to underscore this impression.

Since a new venture is radical enough, its name should not contribute further to this image. Use the name to counterbalance the inherent instability of your venture. The current trend toward catchy corporate names will only highlight your conservatism and contribute to your cause. Your customers, bankers, and creditors want to deal with a solid firm, not a high flier. Your name is their first impression; make it work for, not against, you.

INCORPORATION

Incorporation is the next logical step in founding your enterprise. You have now selected your market, partner, and corporate name. Incorporation formally announces these selections, along with specific stockholder composition and title allocation. Each point can be modified at a later date, but this provides your firm with a starting point. Incorporation also creates an aura of stability and a recognized corporate vehicle to develop contacts with the outside world for your beginning enterprise.

A corporation has an independent standing in law. It becomes responsible for its own actions and those enacted by its officers,

employees, physical assets (such as a defective boiler that ex-
plodes), and products. This limits the liabilities of the founders,
employees, and owners of the business. In an age of frequent lawsuits, incorporation provides a degree of protection for the entrepreneur.

The methods of incorporating vary by state, but they are
relatively simple. A number of legal services offer full incorporation for less than five hundred dollars. The secretary of state in
your state capital can give you the necessary forms and fee
schedule by mail. An attorney should guide you in this matter.
Have your attorney and accountant explore limited partnerships,
subchapter S, and Section 1244 corporations; each may offer
substantial tax benefits to you.

You need not be concerned initially about the ideal state for
incorporation. The benefits offered by states such as Delaware
apply principally to Fortune 500 companies. Establish good
habits from the beginning by concentrating your energies on
making the new venture work, not on these fine points. There will
be time enough to attend to these matters if your adventure
survives.

My first company was incorporated as Brown Brothers Wilson.
My wife and I held all officer titles and stock. The company
offered no services or products for sale; yet, this corporate shell
served as a surprisingly useful vehicle to solicit product ideas,
supplier information, and banking relationships. Through this
company we located the primary contractor for the Umbroller,
established credit lines with suppliers, and began our long-term
banking relationships—all benefits that were later passed on to
Cross River.

Early incorporation can also put you in an excellent position to
negotiate with prospective partners. As a full-fledged corporation,
your firm has the trappings of stationery, phone number, and files,
and some business relationships as well. Admittedly these factors
may be of minimal economic importance in the long run, but they
can be helpful in early negotiations with partners.

In addition, early incorporation is useful because it permits your corporate birthday to occur sooner. This can be especially important in your early years when suppliers, customers, and bankers place a great deal of weight on corporate longevity.

INVESTOR SELECTION

Since money is harder to come by than partners in most new ventures, you may feel tempted to compromise your standards when it comes to selecting investors. Resist the temptation and employ the same standards for investors as for partners. Undoubtedly, most entrepreneurs do not have the daily conflicts with investors they so often have with partners. Yet many divisive lawsuits have been filed against entrepreneurs who selected investors poorly and entered into ill-advised agreements during the early investment period.

You should rely on your lawyer to draw up equity and debt instruments regardless of how small the actual dollar amounts involved. In fact, the initial agreements are more apt to be litigated than later, larger ones.

As a result, be sure your early investors understand the long-term and high-risk nature of their investment. Be sure they know your stock cannot be resold as simply as a New York Stock Exchange issue. They should be warned that if your firm succeeds it will need more financing, not less. And they should know that second-round investors will not let them bail out for a considerable period of time. Consequently, they should realize that they must stick with your mad adventure for at least five years, and more probably ten, no matter how badly they may want to sell their stock.

Quite obviously, the risk for new venture investors is substantial. The odds are they will spend countless nights worrying about their speculative investment and never see a dollar for it. Caution your potential investors about this; your frank recognition of these problems will earn their respect and usually preclude heated disputes at a later date. In addition, your appraisal of the investors' enormous risks, and their understandable reluctance at making such a commitment to your dream, may inspire you to give a more equitable stock portion of your enterprise to those initial investors, who contribute so much to your opportunity by their emotional and financial support. This, in turn, would contribute to better investor relations and fewer shareholder lawsuits.

PURCHASING A GOING CONCERN

Most successful new ventures are founded on a good deal. This may involve identifying an opportune segment of a market, gaining the rights to a new invention or production process, or purchasing assets in a favorable manner. Purchasing a going concern may provide the later opportunity. It may offer you the chance to improve your odds for corporate survival by acquiring a firm with a history, even if a somewhat blemished one, and an existing organization and set of business relationships. The cost of purchasing a going concern will, as a rule, be higher than that of starting your own business from scratch; but the inherent stability, personal salary potential, and foundation for growth may well justify the higher initial expenditure.

The purchase price for most small companies is less than you may imagine. The small, slow-growth company has little economic value to anyone other than a growth- or income-oriented entrepreneur. Large companies looking for acquisitions are rarely interested in companies with annual sales of less than one million dollars because this sales base is too marginal to run the acquired firm profitably as a division or subsidiary, or even to absorb it as a complementary product line. The liquidation value of most of these small concerns is limited because the fixed assets are specialized, and most of the liquid assets have been drained off to reduce tax liabilities and maintain the high standard of living of their owners. As a consequence, there is a relatively large supply of these small businesses for sale and a low demand for them, a supply imbalance which creates the opportunity for a below-book-value purchase.

You should review companies that have annual sales in the $500,000 range. These companies provide enough sales to cover modest overhead levels, yet are small enough to warrant a low purchase price. Sales of this magnitude usually involve a book or replacement value of $100,000 to $400,000 with $150,000 being about average. Owing to asset write-offs over the years, the replacement value is rarely reflected in the financial statements, and this may assist you in negotiating a cash down payment as low as $20,000 to $30,000.

Admittedly, many of these firms suffer from a number of business problems or they would not have remained small after so many years in business. Yet their difficulties are often far more manageable than ones encountered by startup firms. A potential acquisition candidate has a proven ability to sell, produce, deliver, and get paid for its products or services; it has an established reputation, work force, and operating system. To the owner, and perhaps even to you, these facts may seem of marginal importance; however, this situation is light years ahead of the fledgling company, which has none of these ingredients.

The specific methods for selection and purchase of a suitable acquisition candidate should be reviewed carefully with your investment advisor, lawyer, and accountant. However, the following will provide a brief summary of points that have guided me in buying small companies.

Selection Process

Most entrepreneurs prefer entering markets they have experience in. The first pages of this chapter describe a method you can use in pinpointing a market in which it makes conservative financial sense to purchase a company. Then apply the following general approach.

A market having less than $200 million annual sales is an ideal candidate since your potential acquistion company will have an overall market share of 0.5 percent to 3 percent, or more. In its particular segments of the overall market, the company may well have a 20 percent to 30 percent share of market. This means the company should have importance to current and potential customers; it also suggests stability, since a substantial market share indicates that the firm has a solid marketing base. It also serves as a strong selling point to your financial backers.

The first step should be to identify strong companies in stable niches whatever market is under consideration. In the juvenile furniture market, for example, I found several niches that satisfied this definition; the bedding, lamp, diaper bag, and wicker furniture submarkets were reviewed in detail.

Each submarket met the criterion of being stable. The bedding and wicker furniture niches, however, were extremely price competitive and so were excluded out of hand. Lamp companies were eliminated because no suitable candidate was available for acquisition; the two major ones were comfortably owned and managed as cash cows by their parent companies. The other competitors were too small and weak to be of much economic value. The one remaining submarket, diaper bags, proved to have several promising candidates, and I selected one.

The company I purchased had less than $750,000 in annual sales, a break-even financial picture, and little recent marketing innovation. Owing to asset write-offs over the years, the book value greatly understated what it would cost to replace the company's actual assets. As a result, the cash down payment required was relatively small and the payout extended.

The integrity of the owner is critical to the success of an acquisition and to the transition to new management. Almost no purchase of a company can work if the relationship between the owner and buyer is not based on honesty and goodwill. Immediately after closing, a dishonest owner can steal the company's assets right back from underneath the new management. Similarly, the seller should be a person of goodwill because circumstances often change so rapidly in small companies that you may, based on new developments in the business environment, have to modify the contract. As a result, I strongly recommend not buying, no matter how appetizing the deal appears, unless you are working with an individual of integrity and honor.

The following elements of the company should be reviewed carefully before going further. The *balance sheet* should reflect a net worth of at least $50,000; a negative net worth is almost impossible to contend with for an entrepreneur acquiring a new company. A break-even *income statement* may prove acceptable. Annual losses of more than $25,000 are normally too burdensome to turn around. In between these figures you must make a cautious judgment; purchasing a company losing money is fraught with obvious and hidden dangers. In this analysis consider the owner's salary as a normal expense of doing business; do not let the seller entice you into adding it back to the profits of the company.

Fixed assets can be an enormous cash drain in any new enterprise. Be sure that current facilities and equipment have at least three years of life without major repairs or purchases; otherwise, your new firm may become suffocated by burdensome capital investments when you desperately need the money for working capital. *Fixed expenses* should be carefully examined because they can be easily hidden. If, given the sales levels of the company, overhead expenditures are relatively high, be careful; these expenses are difficult to cope with in a small company and suggest serious related problems. In your analysis, pay special attention to debt loads, lease payments, and any accompanying restrictions by financial companies.

Perhaps the most sensitive and unknown issue is the *customer base*. You desperately need the old seller's assistance in preserving it; however, even an honest seller rarely has an unbiased view of his or her customers. So be sure you review this matter closely, especially if the customer base is narrow. Be certain customer base is diverse enough to survive a lost account or two when ownership changes hands. The final factor is *operations flow*. An efficient operation is not as important at first as a stable work flow, although the two issues are usually related. Without an established and effective routine, the prospective company may be very difficult to manage for a newcomer.

Make sure each of these factors is acceptable before proceeding. The seller may attempt to distract you by pointing out the special capabilities of the company; however, if these basics are not in order, you will never be able to capitalize on the firm's specialized talents.

Base the final judgment on instinct. If you feel at all ambivalent about the purchase, do not conclude the deal. As suggested earlier, your intuition can sense problems before your intellect has the opportunity to clarify them. If you feel comfortable with the situation at this stage, proceed carefully into the final negotiations.

Negotiations

Entire books are written on this subject alone. Yet they tend to obscure an important truth, that overnegotiation can kill even the best deal or create permanent resentment if it does not. My basic strategy is to write down the acceptable parameters of the potential acquisition, and if the owner's demands are close, I usually proceed. If not, I pass on the acquisition.

When a seller's entire offer is on the table, presuming the demands are close to what you are willing to pay, make an overall assessment. If you can see your way to accepting it with little modification, do so. The little you lose may be more than made up by the goodwill created between the two of you. Because now comes the difficult part—the seller's lawyer.

Many lawyers can make you suspicious of George Washington's integrity. The owner's lawyer undoubtedly will fit this pattern and plant feelings of dissatisfaction and discord in his or her client's mind, maintaining that the client is not receiving sufficient protection. Why do lawyers take this approach? Primarily, I think, because in this kind of transaction between two small, relatively weak business people, legal agreements are difficult to enforce. Both parties simply do not have the net worth to enforce, or have enforced against them, the restrictive provisions of the contract. This means, in effect, that the agreement is a statement of principles more than a strict, enforceable contract. This is not always the case, of course, but it is in most situations.

Despite the weakness of the final agreement, though, the lawyer will undoubtedly introduce the subject of personal guarantees, salary and compensation limitations, stock escrow and transfer restrictions, and other assorted restraints on your conduct and peace of mind. It is rarely of any use to argue that these restrictions will only alienate you and encourage distrust on both sides; most lawyers believe in the sanctity of the document, even when it has little practical value. You must contain your impatience and try to modify the more restrictive covenants. If you find them too upsetting or limiting, pass on the acquisition; if not, grit your teeth and sign it. Further discussions will only create more difficulties and jeopardize the transaction.

Final Thoughts: Watch Out!

In my experience, it is far easier to enter than withdraw from a purchase agreement. Be absolutely certain you want the deal before signing your life away, since that is precisely what personal guarantees do. The decision is a very trying one. Search your mind carefully before plunging in, and if you get cold feet at the last minute, do not sign the agreement.

OFFICE

It is commonly thought that an office is ideally located away from your home address. Most believe this makes a venture appear more businesslike to the outside world. In fact, assuming you start your enterprise from scratch, a new office is usually an unproductive drain on precious cash resources. Few business associates will visit and little productive work will occur there in your first months of business.

Consider running your office out of your home at first. The cost of an outside office is always more than anticipated and, in any event, will be all out of proportion to what you accomplish there during the early months. Pass this luxury and use the saved funds to pay a pressing vendor or two.

At Cross River I used a portion of my kitchen until the company was doing over forty thousand dollars per month in sales. As a concession to our corporate image, I installed a separate phone and answering service, and most outsiders took it for granted we were operating out of a normal business office.

With a part-time helper I handled all office duties from light typing to clerking. These procedures led me to learn the business in detail and established good overhead habits from the beginning. The financial savings were substantial, a fact the following chart depicts clearly.

COMPARATIVE MONTHLY COSTS

	Cross River Office: My Home	Traditional Small-Company Office
Rent	$ 0	$ 400
Part-time Helper	50	550
Phone	100	200
Office Equipment	0	100
Miscellaneous	50	200
Total:	$200	$1,450

Fourteen hundred to fifteen hundred dollars is about a rock-bottom minimum to run a traditional office. This is without computing startup costs such as office furniture, equipment, and supplies. These considerations would only further skew the comparison in favor of the home office.

Every one of the five expense areas increases in a formal office setting. When my office was at home, I performed many small tasks at no cost to the company. Extra expenses were not incurred, for instance, because copying machines were not available. Typing, filing, mailings, and the like were done in my spare time during the evening or over the weekends.

The effect of these savings can be substantial when viewed in light of your first-year financial statement. A first-year profit, no matter how small, is both unusual and encouraging to your creditors and financial backers. At Cross River, we had a net income of $5,000 on our first-year sales of $569,000. Our suppliers and lenders were pleased with our performance. If we had used the traditional office in our first six months (see the table), this profit would have evaporated and become a loss!

As a result, the minor disadvantages of working out of your home usually are more than offset by the low cost and potential bottom-line results. The installation of an extra phone, allocation of special space at home, and occasional inconveniences are more than compensated for by the extra cash available to pay suppliers.

Where do you meet those important people? Flatter them and see them in their offices. Meet them for lunch. Use an airline club such as American Airlines' Admiral's Club. They even have special conference rooms that can be reserved with complimentary coffee and a cash bar. In smaller towns use an accountant or lawyer's office. Use your imagination and establish good, low-overhead habits from the beginning.

During your first year or two in business, few VIPs will visit your office. By your third year you will need an office and be able to afford one—if you are still in business. At Cross River, no VIPs were even interested in visiting us during our first year. In our second year, we rented an office and still no VIPs came. Our contacts were made entirely by phone, letter, and personal visits to our associates' offices.

FIRST COMMUNICATIONS

Your first communications are important because few of your business associates will ever see your office or factory.

Usually they will know your firm best by its written material. For this reason effective corporate and product communications are particularly significant in the first year of new venture life.

Your communications strategy, like your corporate name, should underscore the reliability and stability of your firm. All forms of communication, including stationery, product information sheets, catalogs, business cards, point-of-sale materials, and packaging should be coordinated from the beginning. This maximizes the impact of your limited communications dollars. Out of habit, established companies often give their communications an annual face-lift to suggest innovation. Your venture is new by definition and should avoid these habitual changes in communications formats. Established companies become stodgy and must suggest newness to keep their customers awake. Your enterprise, though, will go through too much change and should play this down on every occasion. Maintain your basic communications style for several years, at a minimum, to establish a consistent image in the eyes of your public.

Communications stability became such a Cross River crusade that we used the same blonde-haired model, with the same hair styling, until she became a symbol for the corporation. The Woolworth buyer indicated the success of this strategy: "Yes," he commented to me over lunch one day, "I received your mailing the other day; I recognized it by the model." This was but one example of how her image gave us instantaneous brand awareness among our important customers.

Inexpensive, coordinated layouts are available from a number of volume printing houses. Take special care in your initial selections, since you will use them for some length of time. Volume printing houses can, as a rule, coordinate everything from business cards and stationery to invoices and packing lists. They achieve these efficiencies by batching several small jobs, such as yours, together. Local printers are not equipped to offer you efficient coordinated volume work.

SUMMARY: WHAT TO EXPECT IN THE
EARLY DAYS OF THE VENTURE

The early days of running a new venture, or having it run you, are similar to riding an emotional roller coaster. On some days everything seems exhilarating; on others, everything seems depressing, chaotic, and brutal. The whipsaw effect of these gyrations has destroyed many a budding entrepreneur.

The most startling contrast to organizational life, I think, is being so totally alone. You are alone in your office, with your mail and telephone. You are alone in your decisions and appointments. There is neither a community of interest nor system of support with fellow workers as there is in a corporate office, college, or labor union. When you make the right decision, no one applauds. When you make the wrong one, no one helps.

The biggest surprise for most new entrepreneurs is the way their business dominates them, rather than the reverse. You must go where the business dictates. If a supplier, banker, or customer beckons, for whatever reason, you must comply. In large organizations, outsiders can rarely command your attention so suddenly and cavalierly.

The most depressing element of new business life is that you must deal with individuals and companies you would never choose to deal with if your venture were a going concern. In retrospect, I believe this is the area most painful to entrepreneurs.

Despite the thoughtfulness of most outsiders, you will recall primarily the 10 percent who rode roughshod over your company, your employees, and yourself. How well I remember the one or two independent salespeople who would berate me long into the night when I was exhausted from the day's activities. Even though they were barely adequate performers, they were the best a new venture could do. And I remember the supplier who held me up, disrupted my production flow, and bad-mouthed my company unfairly. Yet I needed his parts, so I bit my tongue and endured.

Many times outsiders justifiably will stop doing business with your firm. Customers may lose confidence because of late deliveries, contractors may doubt your ability to pay, investors may lament their early financial commitments. Seasoned entrepreneurs expect these things to happen. They are different in kind from the unwarranted disruptions and personal attacks of the 10 percent mentioned above.

Most galling of all, when your venture has become a success these very individuals will pretend they built your business, supported you in your hour of need, and were your best ambassadors of goodwill. So when you finally have the corporate strength to sever relations with them, don't be surprised when they defame you to the world for being a Judas who abandoned them.

Running the Business

While struggling through the early stages of a new venture, you must develop a clear understanding of what a business is and what tasks it must perform to survive and prosper. A business is an entity licensed by a specific state to operate legally as a corporation. Incorporation is the process undergone to achieve this licensing. As explained in the last chapter, it is similar to applying for a driver's license except that you should rely on legal advice first—the forms are more complicated and the fee structure larger.

A business must make a profit or be subsidized to survive. Otherwise, the company will not have the funds to meet payrolls, pay suppliers, or repay lenders. Unprofitable enterprises require refinancing through loans or stock subscriptions to cover losses; otherwise employee salaries and vendor bills will not be paid. Lenders and investors will decline further investment unless the prospects for profitability are strong enough to guarantee that their additional investments can be repaid. If they are unsatisfied as to future profitability, and new funds are not acquired, the unprofitable company will be forced into bankruptcy or liquidation by legal actions instituted on behalf of creditors and unpaid employees. Consequently, the first objective of the new venture must be to earn a profit to insure survival; otherwise, all the efforts of the entrepreneur will be in vain.

The growing financial conservatism of the public and the investing community requires new ventures to become financially more self-sufficient from the outset. Very attractive double-digit rates of return on commercial paper, bank certificates, and New York Stock Exchange bonds have reduced investor interest in speculative new venture investments. In the eyes of most investors, the potential rewards do not compensate for the risks involved.

KEY TASKS AND PRIORITIES

The difficulty in obtaining loans or investments places great importance on effective execution of the basic tasks required to achieve profitability: sales, fulfillment, delivery, and payment. Nothing happens in a business until a sale is made. Then the product or service sold must be produced or fulfilled. Delivery must then be made to the customer. And, finally, the customer must pay you.

These four critical business functions can be exploded into an endless number of subelements. Too many business people do precisely that rather than focusing on the crucial priorities. Executives are prone to this failing because of the massive size of the modern corporation and the attendant division of work into small compartmentalized sections. Entrepreneurs make this error because they allow themselves to be distracted from priorities by firefighting details. Executives and entrepreneurs alike devote too little time to judging whether all the work, commitment, and effort moves their business any closer to accomplishing these key priorities or whether they are simply on an interesting sidetrip that will have few economic results.

Self-criticism about concentration on priorities is an important though neglected matter for most entrepreneurs. They love the whirl of activity, ring of telephones, mad dash for airplanes, frantic dinners, chaotic conversations, and other illusions of action. These activities often become a narcotic. As with most addictions, this one reveals a fundamental insecurity about failing: "I am not sure I am doing the right things, so I will try to do everything. That way my poor decisions can be excused by my being over-worked." Entrepreneurs cannot afford these self-indulgent musings. They must take the four critical priorities seriously. They must not mistake movement for action. Each movement must contribute to an action that will have important economic results for the enterprise.

Effort must be directed to these priorities:

- *Sales*: highest price that will encourage reorders
- *Fulfillment*: lowest cost that will encourage reorders
- *Delivery*: lowest cost with on-time performance
- *Payment*: maximum amount at the earliest date

These fundamental objectives are too often neglected during the day-to-day business skirmishes. Print a sign and post it prominently over your desk, "Is what I am doing, *right now*, helping accomplish a major objective?" More than a few times I have been haunted by that sign while engaging in a totally absorbing but economically meaningless task.

These priorities should be broken down into departmental and individual goals. Each employee should be prompted to emphasize activities that accomplish the critical priorities. Measure your managers and employees accordingly and you will be pleasantly surprised by the reduction of busywork and increase in productive accomplishments. The emphasis on such minor issues as stationery layout, purchase of office equipment, and office decor will decline markedly; the emphasis given to answering customer inquiries, typing invoices, collecting overdue bills, and responding to upset suppliers will increase quickly.

As you must be critical of your own tendencies to dilute your effectiveness, be alert to the same problems among your employees. Output, not input or style, must be the issue in employee evaluation. This point was seared into my imagination by the following incident.

One of my first good secretaries retained a privileged position of sorts after eight other office workers were added to the staff and the company moved to a large, modern office building. Among these were two mature, experienced secretaries who eventually began to fault the original one for bad habits ranging from impertinence to a casual work attitude. Their objections had some validity; however, she did an excellent job and simply was not politically oriented in her behavior.

Six months later the two experienced secretaries took a vacation during the same June week. The original secretary handled their work adequately although doing so consumed all her time. The office functioned smoothly and the vacationers' absence was not too noticeable. When they returned, the original one took the following week off. Her two critics collapsed under the work load created by her absence and all hell broke loose: work piled up and chaos ensued. Needless to say, the original one was not criticized by those two again.

I learned from that incident that the most slavishly dedicated workers often do the least productive work. The less solemn ones often are the most effective workers because they have a better perspective on their job. Do not let superficial behavior deceive you in judging either yourself or your employees. Effort must be devoted to accomplishing key priorities, not to unrelated activities merely suggesting action.

HOW NOT TO RUN A NEW VENTURE: THE BIG-COMPANY MODEL

Although big companies are small enterprises that succeeded, bankruptcy would have cut them down decades ago if they did in their early years what they so often do now. Corporate prosperity and sheer bulk usually extinguish any sense of urgency, emphasis on basics, or dedication to performance. In their place, caution, attention to detail, and internal political considerations dominate the decision-making process. This problem is underscored by the fact that Fortune 500 company profits have barely kept up with inflation over the last decade.

The original founders of these firms, such as Henry Ford, Sr., or George Eastman, would be astonished by this departure from attention to the priorities discussed earlier in the chapter. They probably would fire the current managers at their first encounter. In any event, the big-company model is not the management style for a new firm to pattern itself on.

As an entrepreneur, beware of the following pitfalls related to big companies.

Do Not Hire Their Refugees

Big corporation managers are conditioned to the financial strength, deliberate pace, and monopolistic position of the multinationals. They are used to being courted by suppliers, bankers, and investors. Big-company refugees usually are shattered by their first encounter with outsider indifference to the small firm. Some can recover from the incident, but most cannot. No matter how much you prepare them for the event, it seems the actual occasion will unravel their egos. Usually, they cannot function without the status and comfortable importance of the big company environment.

The following comparison between a hypothetical big- and small-company approach to launching a new product illustrates the radical differences between the managerial styles of big-company and new venture people:

Corporate Executive	Entrepreneur
1. Develop a market survey to identify key prospects.	1. Select a few potential customers.
2. Analyze survey and revise it.	2. Personally call these customers and make appointments, or just drop in on them cold.
3. Take the actual survey.	
4. Evaluation meeting on survey methodology.	3. See actual customers and get orders from some on the first or second visit.
5. Prepare survey analysis report.	

6. Prepare advertising and collateral materials.
7. Introductory mailings.
8. Get "contacts" to make "inside" connections with key prospects.
9. Secretary makes customer appointments.
10. Reschedule appointments due to schedule conflicts.
11. Have warm-up calls to test selling methods and collateral materials.
12. Plan followup test calls.
13. Analyze followup calls and start making actual sales calls.

The corporate approach seems to be the avoidance of direct contact with the actual customers. Endless time is spent on planning the sales calls down to the last detail. This tendency stems from the executive-curator training which encourages cautious preservation of assets. Consequently, these people will exhaust you with excuses why something cannot be done. They live in preparation for activity rather than simply doing it. Nothing can replace the economic impact of doing something. Yet big-company people are preoccupied with perfection because they are rewarded for not making mistakes rather than for meeting fundamental objectives. The big-company philosophy seems to be that you cannot strike out if you stay in the dugout.

Most major corporations achieved their prominence by winning a risky gamble or two. With their fortune now seemingly secure, these former risk-taking companies encourage executive risk aversion to protect their substantial asset base. Their conception of the correct executive function is to preserve assets and cautiously seek safe, moderate rates of return on invested capital.

Multinational executive training, then, is the exact opposite of what a new venture requires. Your enterprise has nothing, so you need excellent people willing and competent to take aggressive, calculated risks to build corporate success—as the multinationals did years ago. Big-company training and experience only undermines and dilutes these talents.

Watch out for these big-firm managerial trademarks: pride in tough-mindedness (a euphemism for the ability to say no to just about everything except higher salaries for tough-minded managers), perfectionism, conservatism, well-written memos, climbing up the organization, no biases or loyalties, and bottom-line orientation. The characteristics of the small-company person you want are: pride in action, accomplishment, and performance; love of activity, work, and challenge; sense of humor; humility; high principles; and loyalty.

Do Not Hire Staff People

Staff people recommend; line managers act. Your company will need actions far more than recommendations. Your managers must identify and terminate ineffective people, drop poor products, shake purchase orders out of reluctant customers, press customers for timely payment, postpone creditor bills, and handle the relentless confusion, chaos, and disasters of an emerging enterprise. You do not need researchers, efficiency experts, legal and accounting theorists, manual writers, and thinkers. You do need order-writing salespeople, line foremen, motivated employees, and intelligent managers. Line people fulfill these requirements best, so stick with hiring them. They are usually not as interesting, charming, or engaging as most staff people, but they will get the job done if anyone can.

The acid test for identifying a line person is how many people the job candidate has fired. Staffers and inexperienced line managers will have fired few. Most experienced line people will have been compelled to fire a great many. Your venture desperately needs these capable, tested performers.

Do Not Be Concerned About a Flashy Corporate Image or Fringe Benefits

Corporate image is built on product performance, customer service, bill payments, and meeting your commitments on time. It is not based on promotional activities involving parties, special entertainments, and public relations campaigns.

Cadillacs and fancy offices do convey an image, one of overpriced products and spendthrift executives. This impression does not encourage confidence in your company. Instead it encourages hostility, distrust, and envy. Consider for a moment your own thoughts when entering a lavishly decorated office or store. Who has not remarked, "No wonder the prices are so high?" Is this the image you wish to leave with your valued business associates? Nothing impresses these people more than the modest demeanor of an emerging enterprise.

Alex Goodwin, my Cross River partner, and I fashioned our desks out of hollow doors. Our company car was a Volkswagen Beetle. These details emphasized our commitment to the success of our business and suggested the same idea to our business associates. In every crucial financial situation involving outsiders, these facts had a surprisingly important impact on their decisions. In several instances, outsiders decided the issue in our favor based on this consideration.

Meetings

The executive knee-jerk response to an unresolved problem is: Let's call a meeting, chew it around for a while, and waste some more time. In big companies, meetings are wasteful, yet inertia works in their favor (no matter how many meetings indecisive General Foods managers may have, consumers will still buy Maxwell House, Birdseye, and Jello products). In small companies, meetings tie up key people while crucial priorities are postponed. If you must, call a ten-minute stand-up morning meeting. People ramble in the afternoon; in the morning they have tasks to accomplish and will bolt a lengthy meeting at the first opportunity. Remember that no committee ever did anything. They are like snake oil: they promise a lot, but only deliver heartburn.

Trade Publicity, Advertising, and Brochures

Trade activities usually work best to keep your competitors promptly informed about your product line and marketing strategy. Customers pay little attention, since they will choose to discuss this information in their offices. Potential customers will undoubtedly not even notice this publicity while your competitors may be roused to action. The invisible Howard Hughes approach often works most successfully in the beginning. Your competitors have enough problems of their own and do not want to worry about you too. Oblige them by not arousing their interest. Trade activities are also a time and cash sponge; most firms are better off banking the saved dollars and paying off a pressing creditor or two.

Trade Conventions

Trade conventions are much sound and fury signifying nothing. Spare yourself, your employees, and your company the anxieties, hatreds, jealousies, and hostilities of the trade-show circuit. Few orders will be written, a great deal of money will be spent, your key people will be tied up, and all the problems stated above will occur too. At the annual juvenile furniture trade show, we were fortunate if our company wrote $2,000 worth of orders. Yet, during the 1974 trade show, over $150,000 worth of orders came by mail to our office that week.

Meanwhile, fifteen salespeople, four executives, and ten thousand dollars in associated expenses had been involved setting up and working the show. Worst of all, perhaps, we drove ourselves to distraction and required at least a week to recuperate from our unproductive accomplishments. I now avoid trade shows whenever possible.

Raising Money

Raising money is an exhausting, never-ending process. The less time absorbed in it the better. This activity is a necessary evil of new venture life, but it does little to enhance your basic business. Most entrepreneurs view fund raising as a constructive activity. It may be necessary, but it is not constructive.

Lunches and Personal Meetings

You simply do not have the time and energy for as many business lunches and personal meetings as you might like. Eat at your desk and conserve your strength for the major priorities. Save your personal visits for key accounts, suppliers, and investors. Have the self-discipline to avoid the expense-account lunch syndrome; it is one of the greatest executive time and health wasters. Eating at your desk saves time, sets a perfect example for your co-workers, and keeps up your momentum for the afternoon.

A List of Other Don'ts

- Assistants
- Advertising agencies
- Computers and their advocates
- Consultants—except for one-man bands
- Conventions
- Employment contracts
- Excuses
- House papers
- Job descriptions
- Meetings
- Memos
- Mistresses on the payroll
- Moving
- Nepotism
- Office parties without spouses
- Organization charts
- Personnel departments
- Policy manuals
- Public relations departments
- Reserved parking spaces
- Secrecy

At best these don'ts inhibit company efficiency and morale; at worst they undermine the foundation of the new venture. They are the fatty tissue in most major corporations. Keep your company lean to endure.

Defining Your Goals and Making Your Firm Work

If you are true to form, it will be your second to sixth company that succeeds. The first venture for the entrepreneur tends to serve as a learning experience, a euphemistic term for failure. It is similar to a baby tooth—soon enough it will be replaced by a stronger more durable one.

This should not disturb you. It simply means your first venture is not your last hurrah. However, it also means you must have the fortitude to survive a failure or two and come back seasoned and strong. Your first venture is just the initial step in a career.

Entrepreneurship takes a strong-willed individual because one must survive the inevitable second-guessing, criticism, and reservations associated with past companies that may have failed. Remember in these dark moments that no eleventh commandment dictates that you must make your first fortune by thirty, forty, or fifty. Most entrepreneurs, in fact, create their most successful enterprises after the age of fifty. Ray Kroc launched McDonalds in late middle age. Colonel Sanders did not begin Kentucky Fried Chicken until he was well past sixty. Their life stories abound with early problems and missed opportunities. Most entrepreneurs have forged through similar early setbacks before achieving success.

So do not expect a clear path to success or be unduly disheartened by the inevitable early failures. Do not let the current emphasis of our culture on immediate gratification and quick success distract you from your new venture objectives. And do not restrict and burden your early efforts by having inflated success fantasies. They will only undermine your future effectiveness. Other new venture opportunities will arise if the first one or two do not work out.

Accordingly, your personal goals should be to make the first company work and survive, while learning in the process how to start and manage an emerging company. Your principal corporate and personal objective should be the creation of a stable economic entity. Volume and growth goals should be subordinated to this objective. You should not overemphasize the correct selection of an industry (other than to avoid the wrong ones), product-line evaluation, sell-out multiples, and seemingly glamorous corporate issues. If you achieve your fundamental goal of economic stability, you will have ample opportunity to pursue these more exotic interests later. If you can make one venture work, the world will beat the proverbial path to your door because you will have succeeded where so many entrepreneurs have failed: you created a solid, stable economic entity.

The unstated and unfortunate assumption about new venture planning is that the entrepreneur has but one chance to go for the roses. In fact, most high-growth ventures have been the result of seasoned entrepreneurs, such as Kroc or Sanders, or second-generation companies like Xerox. Most people think of Xerox as a bold new venture that emerged full-blown during the 1960s. In fact, the company first acquired the rights to the Xerographic process in the 1940s; it was then a small printing concern called the Haloid Corporation. Under the direction of the founder's son, Joseph Wilson, the company then began its climb to multibillion-dollar status. In the words of Jean-Jacques Rousseau, "Money is the seed of money, the first (dollar) is sometimes more difficult to acquire than the second million."

So do not be distracted by grandiose schemes in your first venture. Establish your reputation as a sound businessperson, learn how to found and manage a new venture, and create a solid business from scratch. Your objective should definitely not be to set yourself up for retirement or make the Fortune 500. Lower standards will remove much undue pressure upon you and assure your venture a far greater probability of success. After fulfilling these goals, you can afford then to take a long shot and go for the roses. Until then, however, concentrate on first things first.

HOW TO RUN IT

The first objective of entrepreneurial management is to focus your talents effectively. Learn to conserve your strength by minimizing your contact with frustration. Use your employees to dilute frustration by delegating the small, annoying tasks to them. You will be pleasantly surprised how they will rise to the occasion, insulate you from pressure, and enable you to pace yourself for effective management.

When cash flow problems arise, for example, concentrate on your major suppliers. This will prevent you from dissipating your energies dealing with small suppliers who will not dictate your corporate future but may drive you to distraction. Your secretary or accounting clerk can often satisfy these people without your involvement.

Cross River had a seasonal business requiring us to postpone creditor payments every winter. Alex Goodwin and I focused on the top ten suppliers representing 70 percent of our accounts-payable dollars. We delegated the other hundred or so suppliers to our secretaries and accounting clerks. Occasionally we had to backstop their efforts or advise them on postponement strategies, but generally they handled the smaller suppliers quite well, defused their anxieties, and let us remain free to work on our other priorities.

A second step is to admit your inability to satisfy everyone. This tends to be a particularly difficult problem for the strong-willed, ego-centered entrepreneur. Yet this restraint is essential or you will waste valuable time settling old scores rather than attending to crucial new priorities. The most popular statesmen win elections by less than two-thirds of the vote, are panned frequently, and are generally distrusted. Artists, athletes and successful people in general are subjected to similar criticisms. You will be no exception to this pattern if your venture prospers.

Your banker may dislike your newest product and may be

right, since your firm lacked adequate market research funds. Your customers may prefer different styles or colors. They may be correct since the preferred supplier refused your firm credit and would not furnish the appropriate materials. It is hard to endure these criticisms from people who do not understand the adversities under which your company must operate. An explanation would demonstrate your sound judgment but undermine their confidence in your company. So you must keep your own counsel and let the heel biters bite while you remain silent.

The third step is to limit your fantasies of revenge against your presumed tormentors: bankers not lending, customers not buying, and suppliers not shipping. Even if these people do not do business with your firm at first, they will remember your company in its most unstable condition. Above all, they will recognize the growth your enterprise achieves. New people and firms may not have offended you; but they will not have witnessed your early growth either. Your early tormentors have, and they often become the most loyal backers of emerging ventures.

REFINING YOUR TALENTS

The importance of having and refining entrepreneurial talents was illustrated to me by a particularly frustrating experience I had trying to sell the Umbroller to K Mart. I stretched my enthusiasm and endurance to the limit, or so I believed. After several phone calls, I finally secured an appointment with the junior buyer. After he flatly refused to purchase my product, I returned to Detroit twice more that year to be turned down.

A year later, the senior buyer consented to sit in on a meeting with the junior buyer and me. It turned out that he was the major obstacle now, since I had won over the junior buyer by this time. Twice more I flew to Detroit and both times the meeting was canceled: once because of his illness and the other time because of a supposedly urgent corporate-wide meeting. By this time, my enthusiasm and endurance for the project had waned; Penney, Woolworth, Wards, and a host of other major retailers were successfully buying and retailing our new stroller concept. Why not K Mart, I lamented. Was there an inside deal I did not know about? Were they simply down on us? I desperately wanted to find justification to drop the problem.

Without persistence, I knew the opportunity would evaporate. So I carefully tried to reevaluate the situation in an unbiased light, seeking hope to sustain me. First I reflected on the K Mart personalities involved. They were not aggressive buyers but were scrupulously fair and open-minded. I considered the company's priorities and realized the Umbroller was not one of them. We had a fringe item in a low-priority area. Taking some hope from their willingness to see me for another appointment, despite the relative unimportance of our product, I arrived with my enthusiasm and endurance bolstered to close the sale.

This meeting went quite differently than expected. Our retail track record was now well known; the senior buyer had observed our company, our product distribution, and consumer acceptance grow. Unknown to me, several K Mart store managers had requested permission to buy a convenience stroller to compete with similar products in competitive stores. On this visit we received a trial order, and national distribution followed within six months. A year later we had become a significant juvenile furniture vendor to K Mart. As the senior buyer told me some time afterward, it was my persistence, enthusiasm, and product conviction through all the obstacles and rejections that impressed him most. If I had not rejuvenated these feelings before the final meeting, it was clear we would have missed our opportunity. You, too, must be on the alert for flagging enthusiasm and endurance. It is an inevitable by-product of new venture life. Resuscitate your hope and conviction at all costs to sustain the fragile enterprise.

Decisiveness is an invaluable asset in a new venture because it keeps the decision process fluid, ready for the next onslaught of problems. Two approaches are suggested for effective decision making.

Keep the small decisions in perspective and make them quickly. Office supplies, paper sizes, and coffee equipment are not important issues as long as the choice is adequate and inexpensive. These decisions should be settled rapidly so adequate time remains to focus on the important ones. If the issue will not influence the survival of your venture, it belongs in this category.

A major decision is one that alters the destiny of your company. No more than ten to fifteen decisions qualify for this category in any year. In established companies, even fewer occur each year. For the new venture, pricing, plant location, new-product selection and development, employee hiring, and investments over one thousand dollars fall into this group. If you spread your attention over the hundreds of decisions that must be made each year in new enterprises, rather than focusing on the crucial few, major opportunities will slip away and difficult problems will tend to get out of control.

Have the self-confidence to reverse yourself promptly when new information becomes available. The poor information systems of new ventures create a disorderly decision-making process. You should accept this confusion as inevitable and change directions with confidence when scanty information is improved by more reliable facts.

Precision and perfectionism are for factory workers and clerical administrators. Chief executives, even in the multinationals, exercise the art of guesswork when it comes to predicting the future economic climate. Exxon, with all its resources, can give its president little assistance in judging whether the American public will favor nationalization of Big Oil in the 1980s. Perfectionism must be reserved for jobs with precise work standards. Entrepreneurship does not qualify for this category. So if you are uncomfortable with the vagueness of judging the unknown and tend to second-guess yourself, seek another career.

Leadership is a necessary entrepreneurial trait because it binds the new venture together during adversity and inspires it during growth. New venture employees often look back to the encouragement they received during these periods, remarking that the corporation could not have survived and prospered without the inspiration received from the entrepreneur.

When I was working as a janitor at Xerox one college summer, my foreman there recalled Joe Wilson's support and example during the bleak days of xerography's first introduction into the marketplace. "I don't know how we could have gone on without him; he was such a person that you didn't want to fail him. Silly as it sounds, those were the best times. And, you know, as many new people as we have now, Joe still remembers me when he walks by."

This testimony to entrepreneurial leadership suggests the galvanizing ability of this trait. It is a native talent little prone to improvement. But, to the extent you have it, let it shine forth to radiate strength and support to your employees and business associates. Remember that inspiring work is far more successful than demanding it.

Maintaining product excellence often equalizes the new firm with more established ones. Your belief in high quality standards will encourage your employees to better performance and stricter adherence to product or service specifications. Entrepreneurs without a genuine interest in product or service excellence usually see their venture unravel in the marketplace.

Customers are acutely sensitive to the attitude of companies toward their own products. If they sense an ironic detachment, or a simple emphasis on quick profit, they will desert your venture in droves. This is why so many flashily promoted new enterprises collapse in the marketplace. The product or service may have been an excellent idea, but the business failed due to a lack of serious attention to high-quality standards.

Major corporations have designed sophisticated systems of checks and balances to prevent lapsing into mediocre product or service delivery. Your new firm does not have the size or funds to equal this effort. Entrepreneurial conviction must be the enforcer of these high standards. This places an enormous burden on the entrepreneur to monitor quality standards despite the pressing need to ship goods, to meet payrolls, pay suppliers, and clear out cramped production facilities.

Do not let cost-saving opportunities undermine product quality. Your operations people will show you attractive cost-reduction possibilities to save large sums of money. You must police the changes carefully to guard against product compromise. The first change or two may seem inconsequential. However, the third or fourth may transform an excellent product into a mediocre one. Jim Sloan, a Cross River partner and engineering marvel, used a straightforward approach to solving this problem. Every month he tagged one product and stored it; every six months he checked the latest production against earlier models. Frequently he uncovered small variations where shortcuts taken had seriously compromised product quality. As Jim said so often, the real danger signals in most companies appear when recent production is compared to that of several years before. Be sure you, or a company principal like Jim, institute a clear procedure to prevent the deterioration of quality standards for product production.

If you consider this a minor problem, think of how often new products have been introduced and made an immediate sensation. Then over a period of years, the product becomes mediocre, not just because newer competitive models or designs appear but, more significantly, because the original company compromised quality by such things as replacing steel parts with plastic or instituting size reductions. Beware of falling into the same trap. It is tempting to do so, but will only result in mediocrity and set the scene for a new product to overtake yours in the marketplace.

Customer service can be as important to your customers as product quality. Routing information, delivery schedules, and exact order fulfillment are important concerns to large companies. As a result, the second step to maintaining product pride is to be equally vigilant about breakdowns in customer service. This is a relatively easy matter to prevent when your venture is small. But as it grows, customer service becomes less personalized. You must prevent your employees from lapsing into the bureaucratic routine of organizing their jobs to suit their convenience rather than the customers' needs. Impress upon them the need to place the customer first, and follow up your conviction by rewarding those who do and terminating those who do not. To check on your service, poll your customers periodically, asking them to make general comments to prevent your analysis from degenerating into a witch-hunt. Then report your findings to the appropriate department manager and make sure that corrective action is taken. This is a frustrating, never-ending process; it is important, however, because the survival and prosperity of your company will be determined in large measure by the service your firm provides its customers.

Refining your marketing skills relates primarily to maintaining a clear sense of what will sell in your marketplace. Keep abreast of new-product introductions in your market. There will be innovators, as you were not too long ago. Understand what they are doing and determine how it applies to your company and product line. New products usually point to the future in your market. These products may not always be individually responsive to market needs; however, they will be suggestive of new trends. Do not let your pride in your own products cause you to undervalue competitive ones.

Secondly, keep closely apprised of customer behavior. Understand what kinds of products and services they envision using in the future. Where is your customer's business going and what can you do to serve those needs? This is far too important an area to delegate to a sales vice-president. You must maintain a firsthand working knowledge of your customers and their changing requirements.

An entrepreneur servicing the Kresge Company in the 1950s told me an interesting story about one of his annual reviews with his category buyer. "The buyer asked me about our sales to discount stores. I told him and he then asked for it in written form. A few weeks later at a social dinner, I casually asked him about his expansion into the discount business and he was startled. He wanted to know how I knew. I told him my banker had told me, although of course he had not. I then offered to help him plan his infant wear department based on our experience servicing other discounters. He jumped at my offer. In this one step, we moved from being a fringe to a basic vendor. Now the Kresge company has become the K Mart corporation. Our firm has grown right along with them!"

Similarly, it is when your customer is changing directions that your firm can make up or lose the most ground. As a consequence, staying in close personal contact with their plans is crucial. Subscribe to their annual reports and compare the messages. They often reveal surprisingly fundamental changes. Clip magazine and newspaper articles relating to their activities. And above all, discuss their plans with them. Your interest will impress and flatter them. Their candor will be your reward.

Nerve and shrewdness appear to be inborn talents. But one metaphor may help you to use them better. When battling a stronger corporate adversary, follow the example of the American revolutionaries fighting the British. The revolutionaries learned quickly that the better-armed, more experienced Redcoats won all the battles fought in the open field. On a one-to-one basis, however, and in peripheral areas, the Colonials won some marvelous victories because of their nerve and shrewdness. As an entrepreneur you should follow suit and seek opportunities around the edges, not in the open field where the multinationals can train their financial power on your little venture and blow it to bits. Develop your attack strategies around the edges, where the big companies have little expertise. Whatever you attempt, do not fight the multinationals head-on.

Marketing

Marketing is perhaps the most controversial function in a new enterprise. Anxieties abound in almost any small-company discussion of the subject. Marketing people are called everything from geniuses to scoundrels. Their plans are thought to run the gamut from being essential to wasteful, depending upon whose opinion is voiced.

The nervousness about marketing relates in part to other areas' dependence on it for survival and growth. Marketing must determine what product or service the independent outsider will purchase. Every department's survival and prosperity will be significantly affected by the correctness of the selection. Enormous resentment builds up in other departments because of this forced dependence.

Further tensions result from the personality clashes between marketing people, whose talents tend to be creative and intellectual, and small-company managers, whose concrete practical skills are necessary for day-to-day survival. The two types reach an uneasy truce at best. Occasionally they fight seriously and their battles have been known to unhinge even the most stable small firms. Marketing is too significant a factor in company survival to permit this luxury.

Your first step in controlling this problem is to be aware of marketing mythology. Its apostles can be every bit as dangerous as its detractors. The most deadly myths are the need for complex marketing programs, advocated by supporters, and the insignificance of marketing in small company activities, suggested by detractors. The most profitable companies, large or small, usually have straightforward marketing programs and give the function top priority in their corporate planning.

Corporate success depends on simple and basic marketing. This is what distinguishes market leaders such as Procter & Gamble from their less profitable competitors. Not a single competitor has ever approached the success of their brilliant yet simple strategies.

My first encounter with the P & G approach occurred during company interviews prior to receiving my MBA. Most recruiters tried to impress us by emphasizing the sophistication of their businesses. Procter underscored a fundamentalist approach to markets. "We focus on our markets in depth; we look for the basic marketing dynamics, then singlemindedly concentrate on them to achieve profitable results," the recruiter noted. "We limit our efforts; our competitors can confuse themselves and the consumer with their intricate programs and shotgun promotional approaches."

The first sign of a weak marketing program is one that tries to accomplish too much and therefore fragments its efforts so that little is achieved. P & G never makes that mistake. Their recruiter was the first corporate manager to introduce me to this idea of focused marketing. And the most successful companies I have encountered since use a similar marketing strategy. In your new venture, keep a straightforward plan in mind. Do not be distracted by complex, involved approaches.

THE MARKETING TASK

A business must produce a product or service an independent outsider will pay for. Otherwise the business will simply not survive. As described in Chapter 2, marketing is the function that should determine what the market should be and then selects the specific products or services needed by your prospective customers.

Before selecting a product or service for the determined market, you must first evaluate the needs of the customers in that marketplace. These customers will reward your firm in proportion to their satisfaction with the marketing programs offered them. Ultimately your customers and noncustomers will determine the financial results of your business by their purchasing, or non-purchasing, behavior.

THE CUSTOMER

In many industries the customer is misunderstood. This is especially true in small, ingrown markets where companies have drunk their own bath water for so long that they have convinced themselves of the truthfulness of their own biases. Vendors plan products according to what they think the customer should, rather than does, want. This is always the great entrepreneurial marketing opportunity: to provide customers with what they want, not with what marketplace vendors decide to sell them. In most markets, the vendor assumptions about product characteristics, market knowledge, competition, and corporate importance are wrong. Your challenge is to develop products, programs, and services that fulfill customers' true needs.

Customers rarely value what suppliers think. Vendors take their strengths for granted and undervalue them, do not understand their weaknesses and accordingly promote them, and remain totally ignorant of customer purchasing behavior. At Cross River we fell into the same trap. We believed our retailers bought our products because of their innovation, quality, and consumer acceptance. An independent marketing study revealed a totally different set of purchasing dynamics. The trade supported our company *despite* various product problems related to newness and quality (our supposed strengths!) because we kept our competitors on their toes and inspired them to better performance. Instead of being an industry leader Cross River was considered the market enforcer!

The company used this rather startling news with major potential customers by capitalizing on their sense of our strengths. Now we encouraged customers to buy because we would keep the competition honest if they would give us the purchase orders we needed to stay in business. With this new marketing approach based on customer perceptions rather than on our own assumptions, several formerly skeptical retailers responded positively and gave us important new listings.

The simplest way for your firm to capitalize on this situation is to speak directly with your customers. They will be flattered, responsive, and pleased by your interest. Most of them will go out of their way to assist you in meeting their needs.

In the juvenile furniture industry, our competitors believed stroller users preferred durability to convenience. Despite the rapid sales growth of our Umbroller stroller, most of these people stuck by their convictions for years. Yet consumers from the beginning willingly stated their need for convenience strollers to solve their baby transportation problems. Our competitors simply avoided this crucial source of information and stuck with their entrenched assumptions about consumer behavior. The knowledge was readily available to any interested questioner. Be sure you keep an open mind to these opportunities in your own market.

In most markets, competition is defined both too broadly and too narrowly. The automotive industry thinks all cars compete with each other for the consumer's dollar, yet BMWs do not compete with Honda Civics. This market definition is too broad, since BMWs compete principally in the luxury market. But BMWs *do* compete with European vacations for the consumer dollar in the luxury market. Not to recognize this fact is to define BMW competition too narrowly.

In the juvenile furniture market, our competitors considered strollers and baby carriages as similar products and classified them in the "wheel goods" product segment. Our research showed that carriage sales had little impact on stroller sales; but sales of baby backpacks and infant carriers did have a significant influence. We defined our sense of competition accordingly and introduced a revolutionary baby backpack to capitalize on our market franchise and blunt competitive inroads.

Most products and companies are relatively unimportant to their customers. Most firms delude themselves by imagining they are important to their industry, marketplace, and consumer franchise. In most instances, nothing could be further from the truth. Giant W. T. Grant liquidated with hardly a consumer ripple. However, suppliers, lenders, and employees writhed in agony because Grant was their customer. Losing a key account is a traumatic experience; to a customer, losing a supplier is of little consequence.

Accepting this rather unpleasant truth will give your firm a decided edge over most competitors. The resulting humility will impress your customers and make you work harder to keep their business.

CONSUMER PROFILE

In many markets, the new venture must sell both a customer or distributor (such as a retailer) and then the ultimate consumer (who buys the product at a retail or wholesale outlet). In both cases you must consider your product selection in terms of consumer needs.

Three categories of objectives influence consumer behavior: needs, goals, and problems. Needs are the most fundamental since they are inborn and resistant to change. Social acceptance is a common consumer need. Goals are the tangible measures taken to fulfill these needs. People often join social groups as a means to gain social acceptance. This is an example of meeting the need for social acceptance by accomplishing the goal of joining a club. The product purchased to join the club could well be a stylish baby carriage which is in fashion with the members. The product is not particularly important in itself; its importance lies in meeting the goal of gaining social acceptance.

Consumers purchase products or services (in this instance, the baby stroller) to fulfill the needs (social acceptance) and goals (joining the club) by solving problems (how to gain admittance to the social club). Products are thus a means to meet a consumer's goal. The products themselves have little meaning to the consumer. It is the end they serve that is important. This may not seem particularly flattering to entrepreneurial pride, but it is an essential concept to be mastered to insure the correct marketing focus.

In this perspective, consumer behavior is highly explainable. It is not haphazard or random as some commentators suggest. Purchase selection is intentional behavior to satisfy specific needs and overcome identified problems. If consumer behavior appears irrational in your intended marketplace, it is only because you do not understand it.

Consider the baby-carriage buyer referred to earlier. His or her purchase behavior may seem impractical and irrational, since the carriage may be too cumbersome for the apartment. However, this behavior becomes readily explainable once you understand that the need for social group acceptance is greater than the need for convenience.

In evaluating your product concept, note that there are three basic categories of needs. Utilitarian needs are the practical ones necessary for existence. These include such items as fuel oil, bread, and housing. Social needs relate to acceptance by others, such as the needs shown by the hypothetical baby-carriage buyer. Psychological needs involve one's self-concept; perfume and beer-brand choices often relate to fulfilling this need.

With your potential product in mind, you should now formulate a basic consumer profile based on your information about potential consumer needs, goals, and problems. This profile should be further refined as your product matures in the marketplace and your firm has actual rather than projected responses to these items. Your information sources will improve dramatically as your venture progresses as long as industry and personal biases do not undermine your vision.

Our first baby stroller consumer profile was quite crude, but very helpful in defining our initial marketing strategy. It also differed substantially from the one designed three years later.

First Profile	Profile: Three Years Later
• *Who*: mothers 18 to 34 years old	• Grandmothers'/recent parents' crucial influences on mothers' 18 to 34 purchasing habits
• *What*: wheel goods product	• Convenience all-purpose baby transports
• *When*: spring/summer purchase	• Year-round purchase
• *Where*: department/specialty stores	• Discount/variety stores
• *Why*: (1) appearance; (2) function	• (1) function; (2) appearance

Our initial profile was correct as a beginning but inaccurate as a conclusion about stroller consumer behavior. In most cases mothers did make the actual purchase, as we originally thought; but their preferences were conditioned by former users. Mothers often purchased the product in the wheel-goods department, but they considered strollers all-purpose baby transporters like infant carriers or backpacks and not in competition with baby carriages or in the wheel-goods market. Strollers were purchased primarily in the spring and summer months and in department or specialty stores. But this pattern was due to product unavailability in the fall and winter months and at discount and variety stores.

Our refined consumer profile was invaluable in perfecting and refocusing our marketing efforts. Advertising was geared toward experienced users rather than new mothers. The product was demonstrated with emphasis on function rather than appearance and as an all-purpose transporter, not just a wheel-goods product. Our sales and promotional efforts encouraged fall-winter and discount-variety store distribution. The sales increases were remarkable and surprised even us. Market share accumulated like a snowball rolling down a hill.

PRODUCT CONCEPTS AND
NEW VENTURE FAILURES

A common problem in most new ventures is a faulty product concept. Before evaluating your concept in detail, consider whether it has one of the following flaws:

* *Unneeded*: Nice idea, but the consumer can live without it. Examples: special-purpose and gadget products.
* *Overpriced*: Better product than competitive ones, but too highly priced to warrant the cost to the consumer. Examples: specialty services or restaurants.
* *Readily duplicated*: Can be copied too quickly by the competition. Examples: many consumer products.
* *Insufficient market*: The potential sales level for your product is too small to support the overhead required to run your firm. Examples: innumerable products and services qualify for this indictment.
* *Can't be done*: Good product idea but it cannot be practically manufactured. Examples: most drawing-board ideas and scientific products are vulnerable to this flaw.

Despite the critical importance of having a sound product concept, many first-time entrepreneurs breeze by this consideration and blindly assume their product's validity. A sound product concept will significantly enhance your new venture's prospects for survival. Venture capital firms consider that 80 percent to 90 percent of their investment failures relate to marketing and sales problems resulting from faulty product concepts. These firms screen out most companies before selecting the few they invest in, and normally their investments are made only in companies with a two- or three-year history. If these experienced investors err so frequently in evaluating product concepts, you should certainly give it high priority.

Many things can undermine new venture survival, but a sound product is one of the few that can make it a success. Your enterprise stands an excellent chance of prospering with a valid and marketable concept and will surely fail without one. Concentrate your attention accordingly.

PRODUCT SELECTION

After an appropriate market has been identified, customer requirements evaluated, and consumer profile established, it is time to refine your concept into a marketable product or service. Your first product is especially important, since it must carry your new venture through its most vulnerable years. You can hardly afford a long shot, since the enterprise itself is one. Established companies can introduce and maintain marginal products. New firms do not have this luxury since the initial product must be sold despite its vulnerability to competitive ones made by established companies.

Your company requires a stable customer base, a predictable order pattern, and a high degree of market acceptance to reduce new venture risks. Yet despite these needs, entrepreneurs tend to compound their probability of failure by selecting high-risk first products, the misguided assumption being that they are risking everything anyway so why not roll the dice on the product and go for broke. The appropriate logic is that you are risking too much already and the entrepreneurial function should be to minimize risk wherever possible. You are already holding on to the cliff with one hand—no need to demonstrate your prowess further by dangling by one finger!

Apart from this warning, new-product selection should follow the classic doctrines of sound marketing thinking. The first step is to establish a market and product-selection chart for your proposed product or service concept, similar to the stroller chart shown here.

The market and product should be divided into three groupings. The different headings should relate primarily to probabilities of success and occurrence; in other words, the least risky are existing products or markets. The medium risk relates to modified products or predictable markets. The high-risk areas are inventions and pioneering markets. The following chart demonstrates the multiplied risk of pursuing unknown products and markets.

Market/Product Selection Chart

| | PRODUCT | | |
Market	*Existing*	*Modification*	*Unique*
Existing	A. Cheaper stroller	B. New improved stroller	E. Stickfolding stroller
Predictable	C. Pet stroller	D. Pet stroller and storage bin	H. Pet nursery
Possible	F. Zoo animal walker	G. Motorized animal walker	I. Remote control animal walker

The Odds for Success

| | PRODUCT | | |
Market	*Existing*	*Modification*	*Unique*
Existing	A. 1–1	B. 2–1	F. 10–1
Predictable	C. 2–1	D. 4–1	H. 20–1
Possible	E. 10–1	G. 20–1	I. 100–1

The product selection chart suggests that boxes A to D represent the best choices with some consideration given to E and F. Boxes G, H, and I are clearly unacceptable risks for most new ventures. Yet all too many enterprises are launched in these high-risk categories. Avoid this mistake if you possibly can.

Box A is often unacceptable because "me-too" products compete principally on a price basis and combine low customer interest with low profit margins, although special situations occasionally make this choice very attractive. This can occur when a major company seeks a new or second source. A new company can be started in this situation if profit margins are sufficient to permit corporate survival. Numerous new companies have been started in the automotive supply market; however, this kind of business is extremely vulnerable to customer vagaries. Without a special and firm customer relationship, the rigid price ceilings can strangle your venture.

Boxes E and F are possibilities if sufficient market research suggests that customers and consumers will react quickly and favorably to your new product concept. The Umbroller stroller was such an innovation. Similar products had enjoyed success in Europe, and in the juvenile furniture market innovation usually appears first in Europe. This made the Umbroller concept seem closer to Box B (the new, improved product), which made it an acceptable risk in our minds. However, without this type of substantial market endorsement, your product may be too far ahead of its time and thus will not receive the immediate customer response required by a new venture. This makes the E and F categories dangerous for new firms. If such products suffer initial setbacks and losses, it is always tempting to invest more money hoping the market will catch up with your innovation.

Most successful new ventures have been launched with products in categories B, C, or D. Many successful new retail concepts fit this category. They capitalize on popular trends and focus on them in the way they are presented to the consumer. Soup-and-salad restaurants capitalize on young adults' interests in light food, wine, and low-cost meals. Since much restaurant competition is neighborhood-based rather than national in scope, these operations can be successfully launched on a new twist. If the innovation is not substantial, though, such new enterprises can be vulnerable to minor changes by their entrenched competitors. This is the principal risk in these areas for a new venture. However, solid consumer acceptance of the product concept from the beginning usually makes this the most attractive category for new venture entry.

PRODUCT POSITIONING

Your product or service must have a clear reason for being. You should describe your product strategy in two or three succinct, clearly written sentences. The Umbroller stroller strategy, for example, was: "The Umbroller stroller will provide the parent with convenient portable baby transportation; it shall be moderately priced to appeal to the mass market."

This product positioning defined both what the product was and was not. It dictated that we concentrate on convenience, not durability; it suggested distribution to mass merchants, not specialty or department store retailers. It avoided fashion or upscale consumer emphasis. And it permitted Cross River to concentrate all sales and marketing activities in these limited markets for results. A limited product strategy makes your product appeal to a defined consumer group, provided there is a reasonable product-benefit match. It tailors your product or service to your targeted consumer group. A broad strategy will include more possible purchasing targets, but the less defined focus will make the product or service mean little to anyone.

PRICING, PACKAGING, AND PROMOTION

These marketing issues should be treated no differently than they would be in a major corporation. If you are unversed in these facets of marketing thinking, reading a book or two on the subject will not overcome this deficiency. In fact, I would suggest again that you follow the advice in Chapter 1 to have a marketing partner in your business if you do not feel comfortable in this crucial area.

PUBLIC RELATIONS

Once your marketing plans have been completed, your firm must communicate with your potential customers so they will purchase your product or service. Public relations, advertising, and market research each plays an important role in this process.

At first, most entrepreneurs think of television and print advertising as the logical means to accomplish this objective. After all, they often muse, these are the most effective media. But they are also prohibitively expensive for most startup companies. This fact compels most new ventures to use more imaginative and less costly communication devices.

As a result, most new firms rely on public relations activities to reach their desired audience. This function is generally differentiated from advertising on the basis of cost; public relations' activities tend to be free (although public relations firms certainly are not), whereas advertising is paid for.

In startup situations, the most effective public relations ideas are usually the simplest and most obvious. The essential task should be to let your potential customers know your firm is open for business, as well as your location and terms of sale. Despite the seemingly obvious nature of this requirement, most new and small companies do a poor job communicating these basics to their potential customers.

A new restaurant or retailer should periodically let its neighbors know these facts. To induce trial, special offers can be included in circulars to promote customer interest. Yet most new firms open with a splash of expensive advertising and little routine public relations followup.

One such instance occurred in a twenty-story New York City office building in which I had leased space for one of my ventures. Three travel agencies and two restaurants also occupied the building. Each of them advertised extensively in local periodicals. Yet not one contacted its fellow building tenants with a circular, phone call, or personal visit. We were the logical audience, yet we were completely overlooked for seemingly more ambitious objectives.

When Cross River opened its first formal office in Westchester County, a nearby deli owner stopped by and introduced himself and his services. He offered various specials to our employees and an opening-day treat for us all. As a result, we tended to use his deli whenever the occasion arose for as long as we were neighbors. In addition, his friendliness and goodwill led us to recommend his deli to corporate neighbors who moved in after us.

Another helpful approach is to contact your local (or national, if your firm is nationwide) media to run editorial features periodically on your products or services. Most media are on the lookout for this kind of information. Entrepreneurial stories are also of interest as upbeat news. Many local papers, magazines, and TV shows gave the Umbroller and Cross River substantial coverage from time to time.

These efforts will be largely in vain unless you coordinate your sales work to tie in with your media events. Do not go on a whirlwind publicity tour and expect customers to ring you up. They won't. Make sure your salespeople go on follow-up calls immediately following the media events. Send out mailings and make phone calls where appropriate.

ADVERTISING

Most advertising is simply too expensive for new ventures. Selective ads in magazines specializing in your field may be appropriate and all you can afford. Many of these periodicals support their advertisers with a generous amount of editorial space to increase the impact of your limited advertising budget.

Take an example from the juvenile furniture field. Only about 10 percent of the population is in the market for baby equipment at any particular time. The most efficient way to reach this selective market was through two magazines focused on babies and their parents' needs. Because of their relatively small circulation, these periodicals were affordable to Cross River. The editors of both journals made it even more worthwhile by giving our product and company a generous amount of editorial coverage to supplement our limited advertising budget.

Avoid using major advertising firms. Their business is geared for television and national magazine work. They are not set up to work on limited budgets, and they avoid the advertising work most small companies need done.

Focus your limited advertising dollars on specialty periodicals, promotional kits and materials, product packaging, and other nitty-gritty advertising work. Small local firms specialize in these activities, the type that your company will so desperately need done. Use them accordingly.

MARKET RESEARCH

In the beginning, most of your market research will be based on your personal experience and judgment. As your firm grows, you should improve your knowledge of customer behavior through a more systematic approach. New consumer product companies usually accomplish this through establishing a small local consumer panel that tries their new products, evaluates competitive items, and offers reactions to consumer promotional materials. These results may not be scientifically accurate but they tend to point in the right direction and are very helpful in spotting major problems or identifying new market trends.

At Cross River our consumer council was not helpful in detecting minor changes in customer behavior. But it was invariably useful in uncovering substantive changes in the marketplace. They alerted us to the erosion of the novelty effect of the Umbroller. At first consumers were so grateful for finding a truly portable stroller that they overlooked most of the product's flaws. In our third year, however, our consumer council identified the need to upgrade our product line by adding a variety of new features. They also indicated a willingness to pay the increased cost that would result from such improvements. This pushed the company into manufacturing a deluxe Umbroller¯ ahead of our competitors, and with much success.

Retailers accomplish similar results by hiring independent auditors to check their stores and their competition's for quality, service, and price. Although they are quick to sound the alarm when major problems emerge, they are less effective in spotting minor trends. In any event, you should consider setting up either a consumer council or independent auditing group, depending on your business, to insure your keeping up with your competition.

If your company prospers, your firm will need far more sophisticated market research than suggested here. By that time, though, your venture will be a going concern and will have the wherewithal to explore the issue in depth. In the meantime, the small differences detectable by these more sophisticated methods will have little impact on your success. The less scientific approaches recommended here should be more than adequate for the startup venture.

MARKETING PLAN

The final step in your marketing analysis should be to draw all the relevant information together in the form of a marketing plan. Most enterpreneurs associate planning with unrealistic consultants or corporate bureaucrats. In many instances, this bias is well founded; much planning is only an elaborate form of featherbedding and has little impact on corporate results. However, a sound practical marketing plan can significantly improve your chances for survival.

The plan should be the fundamental control vehicle for your new venture. It will compel your firm to organize its business into one coherent document and will be an excellent yardstick by which to measure performance. Writing down your strategy will reveal its inconsistencies and contradictions and should therefore promote an orderly resolution of these conflicts.

Few things protect an excellent concept like approving it on paper; nothing exposes a bad idea quite like writing it down in black and white. The planning process should cull out the poor ideas and base your business on more solid concepts. The final document should become the set of rules your firm operates under until the next set is written. This prevents excessive time spent on reevaluating approved concepts.

If a change is approved, this plan will encourage a consistent corporatewide reaction rather than piecemeal departmental responses. A plan tends to reduce fire-fighting activities, meetings, and general interdepartmental bickering. A plan provides clear direction for your subordinates so you can concentrate on new issues and exception management. The marketing planning process will not give your firm magical results; however, it will be useful in revealing assumptions, defining strategies, and clarifying corporate activities.

The following chart depicts a brief outline of a good plan. The plan should be revised annually and updated quarterly. After your first year in business, you should begin planning three years forward. Planning the second two years may seem like a dart-throwing exercise at first; you may be surprised later, as I have been, at how accurate the plan looks in retrospect.

To insure an effective plan, keep it short (no more than fifteen pages, excluding exhibits and financial projections) and write it in a form capable of measurement and implementation. Effective working plans tend to focus on the basics and sound plausible even to uninformed outsiders. Procter & Gamble's and General Foods' marketing plans are surprisingly short and action oriented. Follow their examples, and you enhance the probability of your success.

Marketing Plan: The Basic Outline

1. Definition of objectives, strategies, goals, and tactics
   a. Objectives
   b. Goals
   c. Strategies
   d. Tactics

2. Background
   a. Company
   b. Market environment
   c. Product environment
   d. Other environment: government, regulatory, other
3. Customer profile: consumer and trade (if appropriate)
   a. Customer/consumer profile
   b. Needs, goals, problems
   c. Trade profile
   d. Needs, goals, problems
4. Action plan: implementation and execution
   a. Projected financial statements
   b. Spending plans: marketing, sales, finance, operations
   c. Sales plan
   d. Advertising plan
   e. Financial plan
   f. Operations plan
5. Opportunities and problems
   a. Invesment opportunities
   b. Defensive concerns or problems

If you are unfamiliar with the business planning process, the best two books to read are *Managing for Results* and *Management*, both written by Peter Drucker. Remember that business planning is not a theoretical exercise to fulfill a corporate obligation. It is your company's game plan. Keep it simple, effective, and to the point.

Sales

Salespeople form the combat troops of a new enterprise. They must get the business started by writing purchase orders after all the marketing strategies have been settled. Their role is especially critical during the first months of new venture life, when superb early sales results are crucial for survival. Without these purchase orders your company would come to an abrupt halt.

To achieve these results, your new venture must have full-time sales direction from the start. Someone competent, you or a partner perhaps, must assume this role immediately to insure an orderly flow of purchase orders. Since these orders are all that stand between your company and oblivion, the sales department should receive special attention during the first years of corporate life.

Your company and product will be unknown at first. No product history will exist and marketing programs will be too new to have much impact on customers. Consequently, your potential customers' basic inertia will work against the efforts of your sales force, and they will have to rely almost exclusively on their personal talents to obtain the sales necessary for your corporate survival. As the company matures in the marketplace, inertia will begin to work to your advantage. The sales department's performance will become progressively less important as marketing programs, product history, and distribution patterns create a more solid sales base. In the beginning, however, it is the sales department that will most clearly dictate your future.

SALES LEADERSHIP

Few people combine the creative and intellectual skills required of a marketing manager with the aggressive, desk-pounding talents of an effective sales leader. Yet most small companies persist in placing one individual in charge of both tasks, with the inevitable result that only one job is well done.

Since some small companies cannot afford to hire both a sales and marketing manager, many entrepreneurs solve the problem by hiring a sales manager and combining marketing duties with their own. At Cross River, I retained all marketing responsibilities until annual company sales exceeded five million dollars. We then hired our first marketing manager.

The sales manager's task is straightforward. He or she must make sure orders are delivered on a consistent basis from all possible creditworthy customers. The attention of the sales leader must be focused exclusively on this objective, rather than on assisting in organizational or corporate planning; nor should he assist in marketing tasks such as new product design, brochure layout, or advertising placement. The sales manager must give full effort to selling major customers him- or herself and directing the sales representatives (or in retailing, the floor sales help) in servicing smaller customers. This missionary or cold calling is the most strenuous form of sales effort and will absorb all the leader's energies. The job demands enormous stamina and persistence, since everything is new, from sales representatives and customers to your product and company.

The individual hired to accomplish this task must not be someone who requires other responsibilities for diversion. The most productive new venture sales manager tends to be a nuts-and-bolts individual suspicious of the chaotic, zealous new enterprise environment. His or her natural inclination will be to bring order to your confused new organization, precisely the talent and disposition needed for this job.

Yet these individuals rarely share the entrepreneurial goals of deferred compensation through stock options, future compensation, and well-paid retirement. They generally prefer immediate income and substantial expense-account living as rewards for their achievements. These traits conflict strongly with the entrepreneur's hard-work ethic and long-range dreams. Do not let this personality difference lead you into the common trap of hiring a more compatible marketing type who will accept the sales job to gain entrance to the new venture world, but will do a poor sales job, disrupt your sales force, and try to be reassigned a marketing job as soon as possible.

Instead you must reconcile yourself to working with a sales manager whose personal goals may be different than your own. This underscores the more widespread new-company problem of needing those managers usually most reluctant to work in your chaotic pressure cooker. The people most desirous of association with your dream are often the ones you need the least. You need the nuts-and-bolts type intent upon developing order out of your chaos, though not sharing your goals, rather than the individual who thrives on disorder and will promote its continuation, though sympathizing with your long-range objectives.

SALESPEOPLE

Good salespeople, like combat troops, tend to develop eccentric personalities, much to the distress of their sales managers and most entrepreneurs. These problems relate to the nature of the sales task.

Consider that marketing, financial, and operations people work comfortably within their own corporate domain. Their work schedules and routines are structured and their environment familiar. This is not the case for salespeople. For the most part, they work outside of their firms' offices. Their schedules and routines are erratic and dictated largely by customer needs. These uncertainties and pressures are intensified by compensation plans emphasizing daily performance.

At Cross River I found myself frequently embroiled in complicated telephone conversations and correspondence with our salespeople. It was only upon thinking about their task and environment that I recognized their need to develop highly individual personalities to survive in their job. Our salespeople had no fellow workers to share their coffee and troubles with, except at an occasional sales meeting. Their working life consisted of disrupted schedules, long traveling hours, telephone booths, and confrontations in other people's offices. The rest of our employees had established routines, offices, and on-the-job relationships to compensate for the difficulties of their work. This perspective prevented me, and should restrain you, from joining in the familiar business complaint about difficult and unreliable salespeople.

Salespeople often strain tempers, aggravate their managers, and seem to devise new torments daily. But it takes these well-defined, sometimes difficult individuals to deliver the purchase orders that will keep your new venture alive.

The entrepreneur and sales manager occasionally make the drastic error of trying to avoid these problems by seeking salespeople with a more stable demeanor. They usually wind up with a poor salesperson. At Cross River we made this error when personality problems with salespeople had driven our sales manager and me close to the edge. We sought to resolve the problem by seeking a more stable personality for our Chicago territory.

The former salesman had been promoted to run our western region. The new hire met me at the Chicago airport and drove me to Aldens, a major mail-order house, for a sales presentation. He made a good personal impression on both the buyer and me. My intervention was required to close the order; however, he compensated for this by keeping good notes on the meeting for our followup. I returned to headquarters somewhat dismayed by his poor selling abilities, but comforted by his pleasant personality.

The next day our accountant, Walt Green, requested a meeting to make a suggestion. Since this was a rare occasion, I listened carefully to his recommendation. He placed the new hire's expense sheet on my desk and pointed at it knowingly. I reviewed it, noted the detail was good, and observed that all the appropriate back-up sheets were attached; this, of course, was unlike most salespeople's disorderly expense reports, which Walt frequently complained about. So I confidently told him, "This looks perfect to me. It is the kind of expense sheet you would turn in, Walt!" "Precisely," he said, "and I can't sell worth a damn!" Having made his point, he left with a grim but satisfied look. And of course the salesman bombed. From that point on, I have hired salespeople for their selling strengths only, not for their executive talents or to avoid personality problems.

ENTREPRENEURIAL EMPIRE BUILDING: THE SALES FORCE

Empire building is a chronic entrepreneurial condition. The new venture sales force frequently suffers from this disease as more emphasis is placed on territory coverage, pins on the sales map, and numbers of salespeople rather than on the quality of the sales effort. In fact, a few motivated salespeople are usually far more effective than numerous poorly trained, poorly compensated ones. A well-paid Philadelphia-based Middle Atlantic rep will generally service Pittsburgh better than an unmotivated local individual. At Cross River the actual number of reps declined markedly as the company grew, and numerous ineffective local reps were replaced by motivated ones from larger, adjacent territories.

THE MANUFACTURER'S REPRESENTATIVE

New manufacturing companies cannot afford full-time salespeople at first. As a result, they often turn to independent sales agents known as manufacturer's representatives. They are paid strictly on a variable commission basis and therefore are not a fixed overhead burden to your venture. Reps also benefit the new enterprise by providing immediate experienced sales coverage, and bringing strong customer relationships to the new venture. Most reps carry six or seven lines and they do not have to follow your directions. However, as your company becomes more important to them, this problem disappears and they will tend to follow your suggestions most willingly.

Development of a solid rep selling organization depends on your cheerleading, company fulfillment of orders, timely commission payments, and sufficient income potential to encourage these individuals to pioneer your new line. Without these factors, their interest will fade quickly.

The size of each rep's territory should be determined principally by geographic considerations. The individual's base city is less significant than an interest in your line, sales ability, and need for additional income. Aside from New York, few cities alone offer sufficient income for most small-company reps. Consequently, most reps cover a multi-state area to insure themselves adequate commission levels.

Once rep commission levels pass five hundred dollars monthly they rapidly double to the thousand-dollar level. Reps generally relax a bit at this juncture, concerned that they may soon be replaced by a house salesperson. You must demonstrate your loyalty to the rep at this point in order to sustain motivation. Reps have been stiffed too many times to believe anything but your actions.

DIRECT SALESPEOPLE

Direct or house salespeople are an inevitable outgrowth of an emerging corporation. Conventional wisdom suggests replacing reps when their commission levels would support a direct person. The implied assumption is that the sales force should be evaluated primarily on an expense basis. In fact, the sales force, like other corporate investment areas, should be measured on a return on investment basis.

Consequently, the effectiveness of the sales effort should be evaluated with regard to total volume and profit delivered to the corporation. The true payoff relates to increasing sales, obtaining higher prices, and securing an orderly flow of sales. When evaluating conversion of territories from rep to direct, analyze each of these factors rather than simply reviewing expense levels.

Remember, too, that in conventional ROI (return on investment) operations analysis no item would be manufactured in-house that could be bought from an independent contractor at an equal cost. The difference between this operations point of view and that of sales relates principally to operations people's understanding of the overhead costs associated with the management of inhouse resources, whether these resources are individuals as in the sales situation or products as in the operations example.

At Cross River, we employed the total ROI operations management approach in evaluating sales performance. The company had superb early sales penetration in the New England, Middle Atlantic, and Canadian markets. Commission levels in each area more than justified conversion to direct sales representation. Yet our sales manager recognized that these changes would have disrupted our most productive territories. The increased ROI potential was limited, since distribution was widespread and pricing on target; the increased return could only come from reduced commission expenses. Since these dollar opportunities were limited and the risk of disruption substantial, the company decided to employ direct salespeople in territories where volume potential was large, but unrealized.

The California market was our first target, since sales there should have exceeded $500,000 but were barely limping along at a $75,000 annual rate. We had made two rep changes in an effort to obtain better results, but both individuals had failed. The third rep was also discouraged by his poor performance and, as a result, was not particularly surprised or upset by our decision to hire a house salesperson. In fact, he assisted us in the transition process, since, unlike a successful rep being replaced to save commission expenses, this man had little income to lose by our change. This cooperation resulted in far less territory disruption than would have occurred in a higher-volume territory with a more upset sales representative.

The use of a direct salesperson, and consequent devotion of more management time and expense to the California territory, resulted in a sales jump to $300,000 the first year and nearly $500,000 in the second. Strictly on an expense basis, the territory was slightly above normal rep costs even in the second year. However, on an ROI basis, the enormous sales growth made the decision spectacularly successful.

After our experience with the California territory conversion, we concentrated on a similar change in our weak Illinois, Indiana, and Wisconsin territory. The area had delivered just $100,000 in annual sales versus $750,000 projected potential. Our previous experience in selecting, training, and motivating the California man assisted the company in doing an even better job the second time around. The California person was selected for a combination of marketing and selling skills; the second individual was chosen exclusively to be the desk-pounding closer we so desperately needed in that territory.

Within a few months, the Chicago hire had increased this territory almost tenfold to $750,000 on an annual basis. We promptly expanded his responsibilities to include the weak, adjacent Minnesota territory and he did an equally good job there.

Neither of these conversions reduced our cost of sales. But both changes balanced and strengthened our national sales franchise and added over one million dollars in additional sales to our company. The strong territories were left intact to prosper on their own; indeed, each one grew at least 25 percent annually.

These changes greatly increased the morale level of our strong reps, since they felt our commitment to them despite our obvious opportunity to try to reduce expense levels. Our weak reps, on the other hand, were motivated to increase their efforts to prevent replacement by direct salespeople.

The rep-to-direct analysis also uncovers a business tendency to concentrate on the upbeat side of the business rather than grappling with the true problem areas. After all, it is more fun to tamper with success than to patch up failures. As with good reps, so with the rest of the business: if it works, leave it alone.

THE CUSTOMER

Your business will be built upon your customers' purchase orders. Your efforts will be rewarded in proportion to your satisfying their needs. You must tailor marketing and sales programs accordingly.

These requirements will vary substantially by customer, type of business, and geographic location. In the manufacturing business, for example, department and specialty stores prefer differentiated high-quality merchandise while discounters and chains emphasize low-priced or heavily advertised goods. In every industry the needs of retailers and manufacturers fluctuate widely. The sales department must identify these needs, meet customer goals, and solve their problems with your product or service.

Consider the problem of trying to sell a major corporation versus selling a small company. The big business has made its fortune. Preservation of assets, service continuity, and maintenance of the corporate empire outweigh the short-term cost, quality, or marketing differences between potential vendors. As a result, issues of reliable supply, vendor stability, and product regularity dominate their decisions. Smaller companies, on the other hand, must make their fortune. Short-term differences between vendors usually dictate their buying decisions. They do not think of building vendor relationships because they do not have the far-flung corporate empires to feed, nurture, and maintain.

Your sales department must tailor its presentations to these varying customer requirements. Too many sales departments, for example, direct their attention exclusively to describing their products or services. Few organizations address the question of how their products or services assist the *customer* in solving *his* problems. Too often, this crucial issue is left to the buyer alone to figure out. The major question in the buyer's mind is whether the purchase of this product or service will solve the problems his or her company considers important. Make sure your sales department addresses this consideration directly.

Consider for a moment your own buying habits. If you wish to buy a living room rug, for example, you might go first to a local furniture store. Most salespeople there would tend to emphasize the technical aspects of their products despite the fact these considerations generally play a secondary role in your decision. More important to you, usually, are such issues as the future location of the rug, color coordination with the room, cleaning ability, size, price, and general durability. Yet most salespeople launch into a presentation about the technical superiority of their products without gaining a clear sense of your needs. Do not make a similar mistake when evaluating your own customers' problems; do not dazzle them with technical facts or service information unless it is important to them. Technical facts are only useful insofar as they are explained and used to solve customer needs. In themselves they have absolutely no importance to the customer, who is principally concerned with solving his or her problems, not with the method of solution.

KEY ACCOUNTS

As in most business areas, sales results come from concentration. Twenty percent of your customers will deliver 80 percent or more of your volume. And of course, this means the other 80 percent of your customers will be of marginal importance. Focus your sales attention accordingly.

At Cross River we tried to sell to every customer in the beginning. We sent mass mailings to over five thousand accounts, and Sears received little more attention than two-store chains. Similarly, our sales manager spread his efforts over all our accounts and their administrative requirements; his effectiveness was severely diluted as a result. Soon the five-thousand-member account list was pruned to two hundred key names. The sales manager focused exclusively on these targets and delegated the balance of the five thousand to our sales representatives for followup at their convenience. At the same time, he directed them to devote the majority of their efforts to the few key accounts in each of their territories. Sales results improved rapidly.

Building a key-account relationship is expensive and time-consuming. Yet the potential high payoff makes it the most profitable of all your sales efforts. Key accounts, in general, are loyal to their vendors and, if no serious disruptions occur, usually provide them with years of uninterrupted business. As a rule, these key customers are harder to lose than to gain. It generally takes a major blunder or two to lose a listing. Even then most large accounts add a second or third source before terminating an old vendor completely. If a problem arises, important customers are surprisingly cooperative and helpful in resolving it.

The first step in developing an effective sales program is to list your key potential customers. In the juvenile furniture market, for example, we found that just ten retailers accounted for 25 percent of industry volume. Another two hundred customers sold over 45 percent of market volume. This meant that the other ten thousand accounts selling juvenile furniture represented just 30 percent of industry sales. These data clearly supported our belief that key-account concentration formed the basis for the most effective sales program.

In your industry, the customer prospect list must be pruned to let your limited sales force focus on the principal volume targets. Of course, it would be nice to sell to everyone, but limited new venture resources dictate restricting efforts to high-payoff targets. The Fortune 500 companies can afford to pursue the small account, but your little firm lacks the necessary personnel and resources to do so.

The simplest way to identify key accounts is by the annual corporate volume of your potential customers. This rough yardstick varies in special cases, such as focused retailers (in our market these retailers limited their sales to juvenile and toy products). First establish your list by conventional means, then gradually adjust it by adding and subtracting special customers such as focused retailers. In very few industries will these customers account for more than 15 percent of the list.

The sources for the annual sales volumes of retailers can be obtained from various trade periodicals such as *Sheldons, Chain Age, Discount News,* or *Progressive Grocer.* Annual statistics for other markets are available through trade journals, government documents and reports, and the potential customers themselves. Annual reports and your own salespeople are important sources of this information, too.

KEY-ACCOUNT FORMS

The next step should be to develop customer files for each of your two hundred key accounts. These files will ultimately contain a detailed profile sheet (see the Appendix), media clippings, and annual reports if available. Each key account should have a file of its own, and the files and records should be kept in one room. For the top fifty accounts use a wall-chart listing containing the name of the customer, the products carried, promotions planned, and date of the last sales call.

This key-account system should become the principal diagnostic and reference tool in your selling efforts. As a compilation and maintenance system, it will sharpen and focus your sales efforts. The wall chart in particular serves as a nagging reminder of all the customers not buying your product. More than a few times that chart has inspired me to make the extra sales call that resulted in a new listing.

The first procedure is to set up a simple three-by-five file with an index card for each key account. Each card should list the customer's name, address, phone number, the buyer's name, extension number if any, and a brief description of any information that may be helpful in the selling process. Completing this apparently simple task will be surprisingly difficult and frustrating, since digging up the facts often takes several months. Once completed, review the card list carefully with your sales manager before introducing it to your sales force.

The second stage involves developing and maintaining the file-folder system. Request each company's annual report. Most public corporations will gladly furnish you with one. Private firms are often reluctant to furnish this information directly, so Dun & Bradstreet reports may be helpful to some extent. Assign each key account a file folder and delegate to a clerk or secretary the responsibility of clipping all key-account media articles.

The final stage involves meeting with your salespeople and your sales manager. The objective of these meetings should be to fill out the profile sheets, explain the purpose of the key-account system, and gain their commitment to the approach. After your first meeting, you will be surprised how little everyone knows about the key accounts. Blank spaces will dominate most of the profile sheets. You will then be impressed with how everyone resists collecting these seemingly crucial facts. This process may be called academic, irrelevant, and time-consuming. The hostile reaction usually stems from an entrenched conviction that selling is an occult art. Selling, even to most entrepreneurs and sales managers, is a somewhat mysterious process. However, it is not a job that totally defies description and analysis.

Perhaps the most profound impression will be how few key accounts there are in each territory. New England, for example, has over eight hundred active juvenile accounts. Yet just seven qualify for the top two hundred national accounts, and, as a group, these seven comprise 65 percent of territory volume.

Despite the glaring evidence supporting key-account emphasis, most salespeople initially resist the concentration theory (though they may blandly support it in your presence) by claiming that small accounts are the "backbone of the industry." The key-account system provides an ideal opportunity for addressing these objections without embarrassing or unduly upsetting your people. The key-account system has the potential to help your company sell in a more predictable and explainable manner. Your job is to persuade your sales force of this.

Opposition to a rationalizing of the selling process comes from long years of not thinking about the subject. Most salespeople have the toughness to endure the various environmental hazards of their profession; but, as a rule, they have not been given the tools to analyze their business systematically.

As the company leader, you can assist the sales force in analyzing the business with the key-account system. Skillful analysis plus supportive behavior on your part will help them recognize that a very few customers provide the bulk of their sales volume and income. Once these facts are clearly identified, and they feel your commitment to reducing the importance of the small account, most good salespeople will get solidly behind the key-account program. The program, though, will flounder if you attempt to legislate or dictate it. The salespeople must understand it and be committed to it, or the system will surely fail.

After the first sessions, you should have biweekly meetings with your sales manager to update the key-account system. These should become corporate conferences of major importance. You must stay actively involved as a leader or cheerleader. Most corporate meetings are unproductive, but this is one of the few exceptions. The meeting forces action, encourages a sense of urgency, provides early warnings about problem accounts, and makes you initially familiar with market conditions. Your personal commitment alone will inspire surprisingly good results from your sales manager and sales force.

A typical biweekly meeting brought to my attention the lack of sales to Gamble-Skogmo. A review of the file showed that the stated objectives of the buyer contradicted those of the annual report. The buyer stressed fulfilling the needs of loyal Gamble customers. The annual report emphasized the major corporate priority of changing the Gambles' small-town consumer franchise to a younger, more modern middle-income group.

On a specially planned trip with our Minneapolis salesman,

I gave the buyer a printed presentation demonstrating our appeal to the customer described in the Gambles' annual report. The presentation quoted the report without making any reference to the buyer's previous remarks. For the first time, he agreed to buy. Both the buyer and the salesman were surprised by how simple and persuasive the presentation had been. After that, our Minneapolis salesman became one of our strongest advocates of "doing your homework" on the key-account system in order to sell the key account.

The customer profile, then, is a perfect starting point for analyzing customer needs, goals, and problems. But its output, of course, is no better than its input. Mechanical compilation will only partially improve your selling efforts. If critical analysis is applied to each profile on a regular basis, the system should produce effective results.

RECOMMENDED SALES APPROACHES

Prepared sales calls are the most helpful, but most neglected, sales activity. Be sure your salespeople make a habit of reviewing their account objectives before each call. The sales presentation should be addressed to limited goals to heighten its impact.

In addition, these presentations should be carefully rehearsed so your salespeople can concentrate on buyer reactions and respond accordingly, rather than fumbling through the mechanics of the talk. Too many salespeople stonewall the buyer and lose sales by presenting canned recitations rather than knowing their material well enough to respond naturally to the buyer's comments and objections. This approach frustrates buyers and often degenerates into one-sided lecturing by the salesperson.

After the call is completed, your salespeople should carefully record buyer responses to their selling points. Based on buyer reactions, new objectives should be set for the next meeting. Without these appraisals, their follow-up calls will not focus on buyer objections and provide corresponding solutions.

Unprepared salespeople are prone to delivering filibusters. Not only does this approach not work, it also can infuriate listeners. Make your presentations concise; long sales calls reflect poor understanding of the problems being reviewed. As your company develops vendor relationships, calls will lengthen somewhat but should never take on the one-sidedness of a filibuster.

In selling, the shortest distance between two points is rarely a straight line. Always keep the purchase order, listing, or close uppermost in mind despite your verbal wanderings, so if an opportunity appears you can capitalize on it promptly. Remember that your call will be in vain if you do not close. The close, as a rule, must be made within a fifteen- to thirty-second period, and so it is crucial to know the precise moment and act upon it. When you make your move, do not hesitate. Complete the job. If you fail, maintain your conviction, suggest the buyer's poor judgment, and withdraw not too gracefully. Above all, leave the buyer with the impression that he or she has made a serious error in judgment. This approach occasionally antagonizes a buyer, but you have to take this risk to get enough orders to stay in business.

The influence of social relations upon sales results depends almost entirely on the salesperson and buyer as individuals. If there is a potential personality conflict, one lunch can unravel a year of hard work. Becoming too friendly can become a disadvantage, especially when you need to press the buyer for the order but feel inclined to hold back. Yet a good personal relationship does help to smooth over troubled situations. The best relationship, in most instances, is one that is close, but not too close.

The blown call is a liability of the sales profession. If you have failed to reach the buyer at all, stop immediately. Ask the buyer how you misjudged his needs, and redefine your customer profile accordingly. Your objectivity and openness will usually impress the buyer. The ensuing dialogue will clear the air and permit a new sales approach on the next call.

Finally, an appropriate point to end the chapter on. Quality, as in other selling activities, must predominate over quantity in planning sales calls. Most good salespeople make too many calls per day, which dilutes their effectiveness. Two well-planned key-account calls per day are usually the maximum for effective results. If properly planned and executed, these two calls should generate more business than forty calls on mom-and-pops.

Finance

Your venture will need three types of financing to reach the going-concern stage: adventure money, venture investment, and collateralized lending. Adventure money is the seed money to start your firm. It generally refers to funds required to launch your company, deliver your first product or service to the marketplace, and finance working capital needs for the first six months or so. Venture investment covers the monies needed for the next year or two. These funds underpin the new enterprise while it undergoes early growth and stabilization. Collateralized lending is asset-based and requires hard assets against which a loan can be secured (examples include accounts receivable from financially sound customers such as K Mart or Sears, equipment that has a recognized value in the auction marketplace, or inventory that has a known resale value). Normally new ventures begin to secure these kinds of loans just prior to their reaching the going-concern stage.

Even Fortune 500 companies require these varied forms of financial support. They rely on outside investors and lean heavily toward collateralized lending, as these loans are judged to have a lower risk, and therefore have a lower cost; internally generated funds are normally sufficient to cover their high risk-cost adventure and venture money requirements.

Each type of financial assistance involves different sources, risks, and pay-out expectations. Your potential financial suppliers differ in the way they qualify and appraise investment opportunities. Their needs, goals, and problems must be identified every bit as much as those of your sales customers.

Financial suppliers have interests as specialized as those of retailers. Just as you might shop for appliances at Sears, you must know where to shop for your money. Entrepreneurs waste valuable time and energy seeking funds from the wrong sources. An initial rejection often discourages them from pursuing an appropriate type of investment at a later date. This is why entrepreneurs must carefully select potential financial sources according to the kinds of lending they specialize in. Most financial institutions do not really identify their own ground rules nor the specific markets they are interested in. As a result, you must define their objectives and markets for them and solve their problems with regard to your business.

The usual payouts expected by these investors and lenders are stock in exchange for adventure money, stock or loans with interest and warrants for venture investments, and loans with interest for collateralized lending. The financial chart below suggests that virtually all new enterprise money is adventurous during the first year. Only accounts receivable occasionally manages to become a venture item during the second six months of the first year. In most situations, no working or fixed capital item has collateral potential until at least nineteen months have passed after the first corporate sale. These facts suggest the financial

Financial Chart (in months)*

Asset Type	Adventure	Venture	Collateral
Working Capital:			
Accounts Receivable	0–6 mo.	7–18 mo.	19 plus
Inventory	0–12	13–30	31 plus
Fixed Capital:			
Equipment:			
Unspecialized	0–12	13–18	19 plus
Specialized	0–36	37–48	49 plus
Buildings	0–12	13–36	37 plus
Leasing:			
Unspecialized equip.		0–6	7 plus
Specialized equip.	0–18	19–36	37 plus
Buildings		0–6	7 plus

* Months defined in terms of company age. Month one starts upon first shipment or customer billing.

vulnerability of new companies and why 80 percent of them liquidate within three years of their first sale.

As a consequence, corporate tenure plays a crucial role in the new venture lending and investing process. The financial community desires association with stable economic entities, while the high mortality rate of new firms scares them off. Once this trial period has passed, however, your company will become increasingly attractive to outside investors and lenders.

Investors have high payout expectations for adventure money. This reflects the risky nature of these investments. The experienced investor knows that a new venture can fail for a variety of reasons ranging from a lack of purchase orders, competitive problems, manufacturing failures, and internal problems, to a host of other difficulties. Any one of these situations can lead to a missed payroll and possible financial collapse. The knowledgeable investor knows that innumerable boulders must be avoided and that just one of these rocks can sink the entire vessel.

In most instances, the combined risks of a startup company are too high to encourage financial institutions to invest in them. The few exceptions to this rule are, for the most part, specialized investment firms that set up new ventures around a proven and experienced entrepreneur; a well-protected patent with a potentially high margin; and an abundance of their own money. These situations are infrequent and rarely applicable to most prospective entrepreneurs.

In most instances, then, adventure money must come entirely from the entrepreneur, investing friends, participating suppliers or customers, family members, or prospective employees. Despite occasional polite encouragements, commercial lenders and investors are simply not in the adventure money business. Alternative investments are too attractive to entice institutions to venture into these uncharted waters. The end result is that most entrepreneurs must rely on self-financing to support their new enterprises through their first two years of life.

At this stage, the entrepreneur can begin to solicit financing from traditional venture and collateral lenders provided his or her company has established a good history. Accounts receivable and unspecialized fixed assets are normally the first items to be financed by outside financers. Occasionally these categories can be financed earlier in the life cycle, but this should not be counted upon. Overly optimistic lending expectations will do your company far more harm than the more conservative planning described earlier in the financial chart.

At Cross River the initial outside loan was sought from a factor (a financial company that takes title to your accounts receivable and lends money based on these assets) in our sixteenth month and granted in our eighteenth. This loan used our high-quality accounts as the lending base. Our new company status almost sabotaged the loan despite our excellent accounts receivable history: less than .1 percent of sales in bad debts, forty-four-day collection average, and 90 percent of sales volume to well-rated Dun & Bradstreet companies. The initial terms of the loan were favorable considering this situation but exceptionally onerous given our excellent collateral base: only a 75 percent borrowing capacity against our net accounts receivable less than sixty days past due with a borrowing charge of 7 percent over prime. A year later our terms improved substantially with 95 percent borrowing capacity against accounts less than sixty days past due with a 3 percent rate over prime. The quality of our accounts receivable actually deteriorated somewhat with .2 percent of sales in bad debts, fifty-one-day collection average, and 82 percent of sales volume to well-rated D & B accounts. But, in the eyes of the factor, our increased business tenure, coupled with our good record on the loan, more than compensated for a slight decline in receivable quality. This experience should suggest the weight lenders place on the age of a new enterprise.

Venture investments are made to put collateralized assets to adventurous use. With regard to investor risk, this places the venture investment somewhat closer to adventurous lending than to collateralized lending. A new company must have a year or two of tenure, plus be fully underway and operating, before qualifying for most venture investments. These investments are generally in the form of stock or long-term debt with warrants, and are subordinated to both secured and unsecured lenders and creditors. This type of investment substantially improves the balance sheet by increasing working capital and, if it is a stock investment, corporate net worth. This in turn encourages company creditors to increase their credit lines to your firm. As a result, the financial impact is usually twice the actual investment. The first 50 percent comes from the investment itself; the second 50 percent results from the increased credit lines from the trade and your other lenders.

Unfortunately, this attractive financing for new companies has all but disappeared in recent years. Most venture capital firms have left the new-company market because of exceptional returns from blue-chip and near-blue-chip companies on the New York and American stock exchanges. Venture capital firms were in their heyday when blue chips were selling from fifteen to twenty-five times earnings. Now these same companies sell from six to ten times earnings and have dividend rates approaching 9 percent. Depressed stock market prices have placed tremendous financial pressures on smaller listed companies. Venture firms now often invest in these established, though less well-known, companies on terms comparable with risky new venture investments of just ten years ago.

In the last year or two, venture capital firms have made something of a recovery. This is in part the result of changes in the tax regulations making capital gains more attractive to high-income investors. It is also the result of rapidly appreciating real estate prices and lack of upward movement in the traditional stock markets. However, as an entrepreneur, you should recognize that this situation could change again just as quickly.

In the past, a profitable young company could virtually rely on either going public or acquiring a venture capital supporter. This is now the exception rather than the rule. Indeed, many public companies are planning to go private again. New public-stock issues have become unattractive even to most New York Stock Exchange companies. New company issues have almost vanished. In the ensuing void, venture capital firms are channeling most of their funds in another direction: the strong, established company that requires equity investment but has a very hard time getting it through a first-time public stock issue.

Despite the tendency of venture capital firms to choose safer investments and their tentative return to the new venture market, you should consider them as a possible investment source if your annual growth rate exceeds 20 percent during your second and third years in business, and your company shows a profit. You may be fortunate and secure some of these scarce funds.

On balance, though, you should count on self-financing your venture until the collateralized lending stage has been reached. This means your business will be financed at first by yourself and by any personal financial resources available to you; the company will then be gradually supported by the assets and funds generated by the business itself. In most companies, collateral lending can begin in earnest during the third and fourth years. Your company will then have an established sales and profit record, and financial institutions will start taking a genuine interest in a ground-level relationship with your firm. Many entrepreneurs feel more nervous seeking loans at this stage than at the beginning because their initial aspirations, they feel, have not worked out. Remember, though, that most financial companies would never have been interested in your initial grandiose schemes and would feel far more comfortable with the more prosaic ambitions of your enterprise in its third and fourth years. They are interested in solid companies progressing toward the going-concern stage. High growth rates, product innovations, and public recognition have little importance to the financial community. Stability is their watchword, and their overriding concern is the ability of your company to survive and repay its obligations.

Fund raising should be treated as a marketing function. Possible financial sources should be treated with the same care and concern given your best potential customers. It is not a province to delegate solely to technical experts, lawyers, accountants, consultants, or your vice-president of finance. Credit must be sold by the entrepreneur. Prepare key-account forms (see Appendix) for all potential creditors, lenders, and investors. These forms will be just as essential as the key-account profile sheets used for your sales customers.

Credit can be defined as confidence—the confidence the lender has that he or she well be repaid (on time), paid interest (on time), and given more business. Creditors focus on the basic elements of your business. You must give them fundamental confidence in your management talent, product marketability, and corporate stability. To do this, you must understand the creditor's perspective and the importance of credit for corporate survival.

A common entrepreneurial misconception is that credit becomes less important as the new venture grows and prospers. Nothing could be further from the truth. The larger the company, the more management time and energy that must be exerted to obtain the credit and financial support required for survival. The largest and most profitable companies, such as IBM, continually seek new credit sources and financial placements, despite annual earnings of several billion dollars.

The following example demonstrates how growing companies require increasing financial infusions even after they attain substantial profitability. In its first year, a hypothetical manufacturing company sold fifty thousand dollars per month. In the second year, its business expanded dramatically and it sold an average of one hundred thousand dollars per month. This created the following current asset situation:

Current Asset Item	During First Year	During Second Year	Increase
Accounts Receivable	$50,000	$100,000	+$50,000
Inventory	30,000	60,000	30,000
Prepaid Expenses	10,000	20,000	10,000
Cash	5,000	10,000	5,000
Current Assets	$95,000	$190,000	+$95,000

The stretch on working capital, or current asset requirements, is clear from this chart. In the second year, the company required twice the working capital dollars of the first year. Even if the company made an aftertax profit of 5 percent on sales, which is highly improbable during the first year of any new venture, the $30,000 profit (5 percent of $600,000 first-year sales) would still be $65,000 short of second-year cash requirements of an extra $95,000 working capital. The increase in cash requirements created by sales growth has outstripped the ability of internally generated funds to meet them.

This problem is compounded by the tendency of companies to increase the ratio of inventory on hand to sales dollars as the company grows. And as sales multiply, your customers will usually begin to demand more time for payment to relieve the pressure on their own cash needs. The consequence of these two tendencies is even more pressure on your working capital position. The above chart is based on payments on a net thirty-day basis. If your accounts delay their payments just fifteen extra days, which is a 50 percent increase in your accounts receivable levels, your working capital needs would increase by $50,000 in the second year.

These facts should demonstrate why entrepreneurs find that the credit-selling function becomes increasingly critical to corporate survival as their ventures mature. When companies go bankrupt or liquidate because "they grew too fast," it is because the manager or entrepreneur was unable to finance the increased working capital needs. And this is why so many bankers and financial advisers recommend that new ventures establish a solid base before trying to grow more than 15 percent to 20 percent per year.

CASH FLOW IN THE NEW VENTURE

Your first step in financial analysis should be to assess how much cash and credit your venture will need to get started and survive for two years. To accomplish this, use your marketing plan to divide your financial requirements into the asset types described in the preceding financial chart. The major distinction should be between working and fixed capital.

To reduce their financial needs, many entrepreneurs enter cash businesses such as retailing or restauranting, where customers pay cash for services so no accounts receivable are created. Credit-card companies give virtually instant cash for their vouchers, so consider these the equivalent of cash transactions. Since over 50 percent of the working capital of our hypothetical company, and of most new firms, supports accounts receivable, the advantages of not carrying receivables should be readily apparent.

Manufacturing businesses generally require more working capital than retailers because credit terms given to customers are normally sixty days or longer. Actual customer payments can extend thirty to sixty days beyond the technical due dates, an extension that creates an additional cash sponge for the new enterprise. For this reason, many manufacturing companies begin by subcontracting work to gain favorable credit terms for themselves. Contractors will often extend up to sixty-day terms if they see enough profit in your products. Given the pressure of working capital needs, it is often advisable to forego some of your profits to improve your working capital position.

If you can buy completed parts, or the finished product itself, from your vendor, subcontracting has the additional advantage of avoiding inventory investment in raw materials. Gaining credit from suppliers is a treacherous business at best; if you can use the subcontractor and its credit rating to buy these materials, you will find the whole process more expensive but considerably smoother. More important, this approach can ease your cash flow burden immensely.

Fixed capital items consist of all corporate assets with a useful life of more than one year. Plant and equipment, real estate, and licenses qualify for this category. Because of their long-term value, many sellers of fixed assets will offer attractive long-term payment schedules to encourage purchases by their customers.

Their risk is limited, since repossession and resale will generally compensate them for most of their costs. This should be the soundest method of acquiring fixed assets, since traditional financial sources will rarely underwrite these items for a new company.

At Cross River I was surprised at the ease with which we gained financing for fixed asset items after our third year in business. To understand the situation better, and aid myself in securing other financing, I discussed the matter in some depth with a rivet machine manufacturer. He pointed out that after manufacture most of their equipment appreciated, owing to a combination of product durability and inflation. Machines that sold for three hundred dollars in 1950 were in fact now selling for over one thousand dollars at local auctions. It was little surprise to me then that we could finance his equipment so easily. Repossessing the equipment might even be profitable for such a manufacturer.

Calculate precisely what fixed-asset items your company will require to operate for its first two years, then triple the amount and your estimate should be about right. This is not excessive caution. In your planning, you will inevitably overlook the extra typewriter, calculator, file cabinet, riveting machine, or packaging equipment your company will need to service your customers. At Cross River I tripled my first fixed-capital cost estimates and was just about right. Since then I have used the same general formula with a great deal of accuracy.

Your cash flow projections must be similarly prepared to avoid unpleasant surprises. Since most initial money must come from personal resources, optimistic estimates can result in cash shortages and corporate failure. A sound, conservative plan may deter growth and limit the interest of investors, but it will increase your chances for ultimate survival.

CONTROLLING THE CASH

A new venture must pay particular attention to its cash flow. This is done by using weekly cash flow projections. List expected receipts, then subtract compulsory payments such as payroll, taxes, COD shipments, and normal expenditures such as rent, supplies, and professional fees. Try to keep a week's reserve for these payments, since weekly receipts often vary greatly, especially in seasonal businesses. Rigorous attention must be paid to these issues to prevent such corporate disasters as missing a payroll, being evicted by a landlord, or having the IRS foreclose on your business.

An accounts receivable lending arrangement helps smooth out the availability of cash. Without an arrangement of this sort, your firm remains completely dependent on the vagaries of customer payments; this dependency is a major problem for most new ventures limping along on a day-to-day cash basis.

When your cash flow improves, do not dole out the money carelessly. Build a cash reserve to protect your firm against its future troubles. Your cash flow will tighten up again soon enough. If you have foolishly depleted your cash and spoiled your vendors, your firm may be pressed into bankruptcy and liquidation.

Be assured that cash flow disasters can and will occur at almost any time. If they did not, more people would be millionaires today. If you cannot stomach the agonies they cause, do not start your own business. Few businesses have not missed payrolls, lost critical suppliers, or been on the brink of liquidation. It comes with the territory.

Many books have been written on the subject of cash flow. And although some are quite useful, most obscure the primary necessity of holding on to your cash tightly at all times. Remember, if you spoil your creditors during good times, you will suffer immeasurably during bleak ones.

WHY BANKS ARE TOUGHER THAN VENDORS

Once you have arranged sufficient initial financing, you should begin to supplement it from other sources as well. Give early attention to this project; by the time your original financing becomes inadequate, you will have gained experience and corporate recognition needed to be effective in raising money.

Most important, learn as much as you can about the credit business in general. To convince these people to lend you funds, you must know as much about them as you do about your sales customers. As with potential sales customers, the better you understand their goals, needs, and problems, the better your chances for successfully matching your requirements to their situation. Your first step should be to understand banking from the banker's perspective.

Banks are tougher when granting credit than most industrial or service companies because they earn a smaller gross margin and profit margin percentage on each dollar extended. As a result, bankers must review their credit prospects more carefully to assure profitable operations. Retail, industrial, and service companies earn larger gross margins per dollar extended, so they are apt to gamble more in their credit extension policies. The following comparison illustrates the point:

	Industrial Dollar	Bank Dollar
Sales	$1.00	$1.00
Cost of Goods	.65	1.00
Gross Margin	$ .35	$ .00
Interest Charge	$ .00	$ .15
Cost of Money to the Banks	–	.10
Gross Profit after Interest Per Sales Dollar	$ .35	$ .05

Per dollar extended, the industrial company stands to make seven times as much as the bank. It is little wonder then that industrial and service companies extend credit more liberally than banks, or that your vendors are often better sources of credit than your bankers.

As they become less anxious about your corporate survival, suppliers emerge as even better credit sources. Remember that your use of their products or services has increased with your sales. This makes your venture doubly valuable to them as a better credit risk, owing to your business tenure, and as a larger customer. Consequently, the entrepreneur should give these credit sources special attention.

THE CREDIT BUSINESS

Most analyses of the credit business are too technical. Liquidity ratios, current asset relationships, and debt-equity ratios are bandied about. Consideration focuses on mathematical measurements employed for granting credit, establishing maximum dollar limits, or turning delinquent accounts over for collection. This approach has led to an unwarranted mystification of the subject, and an almost complete obfuscation of the underlying credit process.

Credit is used as a marketing tool; it is granted by companies to encourage customer orders. Favored and desirable accounts are accommodated to receive their business. These concessions may take the form of longer terms, cash discounts, or larger credit lines than the customer's financial condition might normally warrant.

Credit—a marketing tool? What else? Otherwise, suppliers would vastly prefer cash with the order to avoid collection and administrative costs. Yet most entrepreneurs do not capitalize on credit as a marketing tool.

Retailers are particularly adept at gaining favorable supplier credit terms owing to their thin capitalization and profit margins. My favorite example of the shrewd use of vendor credit lines occurred with Zayre, a major discount chain. In our second year selling Umbrollers, the Zayre juvenile furniture buyer gave us a test order and found the product retailed well. Soon our accounts receivable level exceeded twenty-five thousand dollars with Zayre, an achievement which triggered a personally signed letter from the Zayre president welcoming Cross River to the exalted status of a "Zayre preferred vendor." A number of small privileges were extended to us, and the attention of the company president seemed to be a great compliment. It was definitely an excellent showpiece for our various creditors, lenders, and investors. At the end of the letter came the punch line: all Zayre "preferred vendors" did business on net sixty-day terms (previously Cross River had granted them thirty-day terms)!

It was a brilliant stroke. Just as a new vendor would begin to develop a relationship with Zayre and feel especially vulnerable to being displaced by another supplier, Zayre applied credit pressure. I learned from these professionals and employed a similar technique on our own vendors. The results were surprisingly good. Just as we had done with Zayre, most vendors simply conformed to the request by acknowledging the letter and putting the extended terms into effect. Other suppliers required a skirmish but eventually capitulated. Only about 30 percent flatly refused to grant the additional thirty-days dating.

At this stage in our growth, gaining an additional fifty-thousand-dollar credit line from a bank would have required an enormous effort and a fair amount of luck. Our vendor extension plan cost us no interest, put no additional pressures on our limited banking credit lines, and freed up over $250,000 of working capital within two months.

After the success of our first vendor extension effort, the company began a concentrated program to select vendors primarily on a credit basis, provided that quality and costs were reasonably similar. A number of aggressive vendors offered us ninety-day terms, an extension that further increased our working capital and reduced our debt. In your new venture, shop carefully for credit when making purchases. Extended terms may be far more im-

portant to your corporate survival than a percent or two lower
cost.

WINNING THE CREDITOR'S CONFIDENCE

Credit managers evaluate accounts receivable risks much the
way you might. They employ criteria similar to those used in the
partnership analysis: character, capacity, credit rating, and capital.

Character, or reliability and stability, means that the largest
company is not always the one chosen to do business with. Rather,
the firm with a consistent record of fulfilling its commitments re-
ceives preference. Many small companies develop just this rapport
with their creditors and receive even more generous terms than
Fortune 500 companies.

Capacity relates to the credit manager's appraisal of your
corporate ability to digest and pay off financial obligations. New
ventures with rapid growth rates are often considered high risks
on this point because credit managers wonder whether these firms
will have the financial resources to meet their increased commitments as they fall due. Orderly growth is more comforting to them
than rapid expansion, as they have seen all too many firms collapse
from overexpansion.

Credit rating refers to your corporate reputation within the
financial community. Good ratings result from meeting your obligations on time, corporate tenure, and a strong balance sheet.
Your personal openness to credit inquiries can also play a
significant role in this evaluation. Poor ratings result from late
or erratic bill payments, chargeback disputes, weak balance sheets,
and avoidance of creditor inquiries.

Capital analysis is based exclusively on balance-sheet assets.
This is a principal new venture vulnerability, since few new
companies have a solid balance sheet. Your character, capacity,
and credit ratings must be positive enough to overcome this weakness in the credit manager's eyes.

Ultimately, though, the credit evaluation centers on the

credit manager's assessment of your corporate prospects for survival. If the credit manager firmly believes your venture will endure, he or she will want to be a ground-floor participant in your growth even if this involves moderate risks in the early years. The manager knows that ground-floor vendors are remembered by entrepreneurs, and these vendors have a decided edge as long as the founders are associated with the company. At least indirectly, then, the trappings of survival will be what ultimately convinces the credit manager. Product acceptance, new facilities, publicity, and customer recognition each play a role in this process. Consequently, the final factor influencing the credit manager's judgment will be the glamor of your new adventure. Creditors, like most people, enjoy participating in interesting situations. As a result, companies such as Eastman Kodak and Xerox had better initial credit opportunities precisely because of their product acceptance, public interest, and entrepreneurial personalities. Few creditors will acknowledge this bias, since they are supposedly bottom-line oriented, tough-guy managers. Do not be fooled; no matter how weak your balance sheet, you still represent the American dream of the unknown with a wagon hitched to a star. Make your case accordingly.

A tubing fabricator tipped me off to the importance of these factors in my first year of business. He had developed a profitable business supplying various tubing products to General Motors. However, all of his products were buried inside a variety of engines. Our business interested him because our stroller tubing would be visible rolling down local sidewalks. When he took on our project he said, "You're the first blue-sky idea man to ever produce the product—I've seen hundreds that never got off the ground. One of the other reasons I like your business is that my family will finally see what I do—they'll see it on all the strollers in our neighborhood!" Balance sheets played little part in this credit judgment.

The credit deck is stacked against you in the beginning. Your venture has no history, stable or otherwise; no substantial fixed assets exist; and no profit history is available. Your venture must rely on intangible factors such as hopes, dreams, and forecasts, and these are all suspicious currencies in the credit community. The impression of corporate survival ability, the belief in the American dream, and the strength of your personal appeal are your only trump cards. Play them astutely.

From the Other Side of the Desk

Credit managers usually feel more like lepers than healthy human beings. No one wants to talk or meet with them. In shutting off customer credit lines, they upset their own sales force, jeopardize the survival of their customers, and waste the countless dollars spent by the company wooing these very accounts. Their task is dominated by the negative; they must say *no, no, no* all day long. And to make matters even worse for them, they view their product—debt—like heroin: one shot and the customer is hooked for life. Yet as credit managers, this makes them the heroin dealer, doling out debt all day long.

Your opportunity is to make them feel more positive about themselves and their job by structuring your requests so they can say yes occasionally. They will welcome the chance to escape the negative. They are lied to, avoided, ducked, hated, and feared. Your antidote is to be forthright, honest, and friendly. Creditors are almost uniformly impressed by directness, no matter how bad the news. Call them immediately if your firm cannot fulfill a commitment. Remember that they have gone on the line for your company by granting it credit. If you miss a due date, their boss will call *them* on the line. Give them an opportunity to cover up for both of you. You will be amazed how well they can do it, if given the chance. Inside their corporation, they are your advocate; do not pull the rug out from underneath them. You jeopardize both of your positions if you mislead them.

When your firm is in trouble, ask them to help you work out an equitable payment schedule. They above all want your firm to survive so it can liquidate its debts.

Keeping the Creditor's Confidence

Give your secretary orders, the eleventh commandment if necessary, that the credit managers of your major creditors can reach you at any time. Small problems will remain small if you respond immediately to their first inquiry.

Be direct and honest, yet positive, in answering their questions. Credit managers want to hear the good news about your company. They hear the bad news often enough. They will be delighted to hear about a new cost savings or customer.

Prepare them in advance for cash flow problems so they can alter their own forecasts. Prenotification will prepare them mentally to deal with your problems and give them confidence in your planning abilities. Call them as soon as you learn about bounced checks, broken commitments, or projected late payments.

Develop a relationship with your credit manager's boss, so you can be more than just another company name. Flatter your credit managers to their bosses by grimly complimenting their toughness, acidity, and ability to pull money out of your tight fists. This respect will encourage both parties to cooperate with you as fully as possible.

Encourage credit managers to enjoy doing business with you. Invite them to lunch; send them holiday cards. Welcome their involvement, solicit their opinions, and support their companies. They can be your best friend in a pinch—in other words, when you are broke!

Finally, keep all of your creditors in the game so they have too much to lose if they pull out. Be very leery of reducing your payable levels; the more they have to lose, the less attractive it will be for them to pull the plug on your company.

How to Influence Creditors on Your Behalf

Experience is the cornerstone of the credit community. All the financial statements, product histories, and company reports mean little to them in comparison with their experience with your account. So be sure to start building a track record with each creditor as soon as possible, no matter how small the actual dollar amounts. You may have to give personal guarantees to gain a credit line. If so, try to limit them to one year, since this should be enough to demonstrate your sincerity.

After establishing a credit line, gradually increase your use of it. I raised our aluminum source from a $12,000 to a $100,000 line by small steps. Our first full reevaluation occurred when our line exceeded $125,000. By this time, our company was too important a customer and too deeply indebted for the aluminum company to take any drastic steps against us.

Use alternative vendors to increase credit lines and protect your sources of supply should your firm have a falling out with your first supplier, but do not, in an impassioned moment, irritate or threaten your major source with this information. Just create this reserve quietly, and your first supplier will eventually discover your second source and reach his or her own conclusions.

Do not let your credit manager associate your calls and correspondence exclusively with bad news. Call your major credit managers at least once a month to have a chat. Discussions with their salespeople or executives do not count. Include your credit managers in your corporate mailings so they develop a sense of your products and have a full file on your business. Try to get your products included in their industrial exhibits and, if appropriate, ask key company people to sample your products or services.

Your involvement with the credit community will gradually increase as your venture grows. Start on the right foot by overlooking the inevitable criticisms and rejections and by not retaliating in kind. Keep all potential financial prospects aware of your progress. If your firm prospers, the ones who rejected you earlier will respect you even more for not shutting the door on them. These companies often turn out to be your most loyal supporters because they have observed your growth and feel guilty for not having supported you in the beginning. Do not be too proud to court them later.

Above all, treat your creditors, suppliers, lenders, and investors with respect. They usually have more money riding on your venture than you do; they know little about your business and so must rely almost exclusively on your stewardship. They will suffer their share of sleepless nights betting on your madcap adventure, so show them the loyalty they deserve for backing you.

CREDIT SOURCES OTHER THAN BANKS

Obtaining credit is similar to seeking new customers. Identify prime prospects and pursue them as you would a key account. The preceding analysis has identified suppliers as important credit candidates. Commercial lending companies are also significant sources for money.

Accounts Receivable Financing

Your customers are indirectly one of your best potential sources of credit. Their purchase orders coupled with your invoices represent a significant collateral asset. Outside financial companies will usually advance funds against your customers' promises to pay, provided your firm has some tenure and the customers have good credit ratings.

Factoring is usually the first available form of this receivable financing. The lending company takes complete title to the invoices and collects directly from your customers. Once these funds are actually collected, factors need not rely on your collection services nor on your paying them. Factoring, in effect, removes you from the transaction once shipments have been made.

Factors charge a processing fee, known as a factoring fee, of 1 percent to 1.5 percent of your net invoiced billings. In addition, they charge you approximately 3 percent to 4 percent over prime on advances you take against your invoices. Your firm benefits from factoring by being able to draw down loans upon shipment instead of waiting until collection, giving the factor full collection responsibility, and making bad debts the factor's problem. The disadvantages are that many customers dislike being subjected to factors, and your costs are substantially higher than self-financing (about 24 percent effective interest rate on loans, when you consider all costs associated with the factor agreement).

Normal accounts receivable financing is much less expensive. Your bank or a commercial lender advances funds using only your receivables as collateral. They file under the Uniform Commercial Code (UCC), as the factor would, but your customers continue to pay you directly. Cash advances are usually offered on a lower percentage of your receivables, but no factoring fee is charged. While factors may loan up to 95 percent of your net billings, accounts receivable lenders usually restrict their loans to 80 percent. The advantages are that you have less cost and paperwork, and your customers are not notified about a third-party lender or owner of their paper. The disadvantages are that your firm can borrow less money, must assume bad debt responsibilities, and is subject to more rigorous lending standards than it would be with factors.

Suppliers of Capital Equipment

Many suppliers and their leasing companies offer generous lease and lease-purchase agreements to encourage sales of their equipment. As a result, the terms are quite favorable and not as restrictive as those of most commercial lenders. This is an excellent and easy source of credit for most new ventures, as suggested earlier in the chapter; moreover, suppliers' credit managers will tend to give your firm a good credit reference to the trade.

Inventory

Inventory loans are probably the most dangerous loans for a company to take. Doing so suggests to the credit community that you are loaned up to the hilt and that no collateral remains for the unsecured creditors. Since a UCC filing is required, and most suppliers and lenders subscribe to services that instantly notify them of UCC filings, inventory loans will send danger signals to your current creditors. As a result, inventory loans should be taken out as a very last resort.

Venture Capital Loans

Acquiring a venture capital loan is usually a six- to twelve-month process from the first contact to the final closing. It is a complex and harrowing process, and a number of good books have been written on the subject to assist you in it. A few cautionary notes are, however, in order. First, private placements have become an increasingly tricky legal problem, so be sure your lawyer is involved from the beginning. A lawyer will refer you to the appropriate legal specialists. Second, do not be concerned about seeking venture capital loans until your business is at least one year old and has over $500,000 in sales. The venture capital loan business has settled principally into investments in small, established companies with prospects for becoming major ($25,000,000 plus) firms. As mentioned earlier, they are rarely interested in startup situations.

Small Business Administration

The federal government has set up one agency that effectively assists small businesses. The Small Business Administration, known as the SBA, guarantees bank loans to small businesses. Occasionally it grants direct loans, but it prefers to extend loans through bank guarantees.

The SBA provides up to a 90-percent guarantee. In other words, should your loan not be repaid, the bank can recover ninety cents on the dollar from the SBA. In theory this substantially reduces the bank's risk; in practice, this does not necessarily occur because of banking politics.

Since the federal government is so intertwined in bank regulation, most banks are leery about applying to the SBA for bad debt support on the 90-percent guarantee. The SBA keeps close tabs on what banks stiffed them for their guarantee. Since the federal government has so much clout in bank regulation, the banks are understandably concerned about upsetting Uncle Sam. The result is that banks treat most SBA loans virtually the same way they treat regular loans. Most SBA money goes to small, established companies rather than to startup situations. Consequently, pursuing this loan avenue is risky unless you have the assets to guarantee the loan yourself.

The SBA procedure should begin by soliciting a bank familiar with you and your business. They will advise you that the SBA requires two bank turndowns before you qualify for a loan. (Since you probably are not in a position to be given a loan without SBA support, your bank can furnish these turndowns.) The loan application to your banker should include your marketing-business plan, projected financial statements, product samples, résumés of key principals, and personal balance sheets.

At this stage a successful loan application will depend on your collateral, the extent of your financial needs, your presentation, your past banking and credit record, and the banker's interest in small-business lending. No banker will seem very interested, so do not be disheartened by an apathetic response. Bankers seem to be sent to a special school for doom and gloom. Most bankers I have dealt with have treated me with seeming condescension and distrust. They have, however, often provided solid credit recommendations to outsiders and have been strong advocates on my behalf to their loan committees. It simply seems that a negative aura is as critical to their self-image as a vice-presidential title. Think of it as a custom of the country rather than as a brazen insult and you will endure it better.

Summary

As an entrepreneur, you must regularly seek new credit sources. Old ones will dry up, go into other businesses, or lose interest in yours. This must be a major concern for you at all times. Pursue it with energy and review books on the subject as they appear.

FINANCIAL LEADERSHIP

As suggested in the marketing section, financial considerations must have priority in market and product selection. The financial officer plays a major role in determining corporate policy because the continual scarcity of cash catapults this individual into a major decision-making role. Because of the importance of the financial task, you should retain full responsibility for it until your company can hire a capable financial vice-president. This function is perhaps the most difficult to delegate and of all business functions the most likely to be retained by the entrepreneur himself. Many entrepreneurs appoint vice-presidents of finance in name but retain the real responsibilities themselves. This tendency suggests the importance most entrepreneurs assign to finance.

THE TASK

The financial task is split between controlling the cash and recordkeeping. Since cash flow issues have been dealt with earlier, the recordkeeping function will be considered here. Of all new company functions, this one is usually the most alien to the entrepreneurial personality. So much must be accomplished in general that most entrepreneurs have little patience for the restraint of the "bean-counters" or for the administrative details so necessary for corporate order. This impatience occurs with almost as much frequency in the educated entrepreneur as in the untrained one. With some chagrin, I remember my own ranting and raving over such details.

As a result, you must protect this function from your own intrusions as well as from the chaos so natural to a growing company. Your outside accountant should be given substantial latitude in setting up your bookkeeping system and monitoring its effectiveness. Sometimes entrepreneurs solve this problem by having their bookkeeper report directly to their outside accountant. This is a drastic, though often necessary step. If you do not use a bookkeeper from the start, one will have to reconstruct your books later—a difficult, inaccurate, expensive, and frustrating task.

Your records should be divided into two sections, receipts and expenditures. Each customer (receipts) and supplier (expenditures) should have its own file, and each invoice should have a check stub or number attached to it. This seemingly simple, though quite complicated, process will be the basis of your corporate recordkeeping system. Above all, be sure you appoint an accountant and follow instructions from the beginning. Your natural inclinations undoubtedly will be to avoid the entire subject. Do not. Correct handling of this issue will save you untold suffering.

NECESSARY CONTROLS

Build financial controls into your marketing plan. These systems should be developed using your accountant's advice. A few specific suggestions, however, are in order.

Checks should be signed only by your partner or yourself. Delegate little buying responsibility except for incidental items such as stationery. Monitor expense accounts closely to set good corporate habits and to keep them under control.

Since this area of responsibility is often alien to the entrepreneurial personality, it is important that you rely heavily on the assistance and counsel of your accountant. Most important, have the accountant help you develop and monitor your recordkeeping and business-planning systems.

Operations

Operations tends to be the most unwieldly department in a new venture. The marketing, sales, and finance functions may require more imagination and intelligence, but operations demands the largest infusion of people, equipment, and cash.

This fact is illustrated by comparing the number of people employed in each functional area. One vice-president, one secretary, and ten sales representatives delivered four million dollars of sales to Cross River in 1972. One vice-president and six clerks ran our financial area during the same period. Yet operations required one vice-president, four foremen, six managers, eight clerks, and over one hundred factory workers to produce the amount of product necessary to support this sales level. In other words, over 85 percent of our employees were involved in operations.

This employment imbalance meant that each salesperson accounted for approximately $350,000 in annual sales, while each operations employee supported less than $30,000. This lopsided ratio continued the following year as sales increased by two million dollars. Sales added just four people while operations bolstered its staff by forty-seven!

Little wonder, then, that the marketing, sales, and financial areas tend to be more stable than the operations department in a new venture. Each member of the other departments has an important effect on corporate fortunes, and this makes them visible and well known to the entrepreneur. The resulting personal relationships and respect usually inspire commitment and loyalty.

Unfortunately, the opposite is true for most new venture operations employees. At Cross River, for example, I knew each operations employee well only when the company was very small. As the firm expanded, I became progressively less familiar with the new hires as a result of the sheer size of the department. For the operations employees this caused the customary new venture problem of having the impersonal atmosphere of a big company coupled with the low pay and poor benefits of a small one: a deadly combination that can have a devastating effect on corporate survival, since many of these employees feel insecure, underpaid, and hostile. Partial alienation of 85 percent of any organization can be dangerous; in an unstable new company it can be lethal.

The problem is often compounded by entrepreneurial distaste for and temperamental incompatibility with the prosaic details of operations management. Inevitably, operations tends to be ignored, get out of control, and become a constant source of difficulties for the emerging corporation.

The potential magnitude of these problems is huge. And so, to improve the stability of your firm, it is wise to limit your involvement in operations activities. The principal operations objective, then, should be the creation of a smoothly functioning work area. Volume, profit, quality, and related concerns must be subordinated to this fundamental goal.

Delegating responsibility for manufacturing or service fulfillment to reliable contractors can save your new enterprise untold growing pains. Indeed, many successful manufacturing firms did this in their early years in order to concentrate on other priorities. Polaroid, for example, subcontracted its instant film production to Kodak for years so it could focus on other opportunities and problems; after it had created a stable base, it brought its film production inhouse. Many startup retailers rely heavily on outside contractors at the outset. They generally rent space, lease fixtures, and buy a substantial portion of their merchandise on consignment, while others use a nationally known franchise to get expert assistance from the beginning. Relying on outside contractors or franchise support permits the retail entrepreneur to focus almost exclusively on a limited number of operations problems. Startup manufacturers would do well to take note of this successful tendency of entrepreneurial retailers.

The principal advantages of contractors are that they shoulder part of your financial burden, provide product or service at a fixed cost, and handle the bulk of the cumbersome operations task. Your firm is not subject, therefore, to cost overruns, dissident operations employees, and excessive management involvement in operations problems. You are less likely to purchase unsaleable materials, carry excessive inventories, or spend sixteen hours a day in the factory or store.

IF YOU MUST GET INVOLVED

Sooner or later most entrepreneurs become deeply involved in operations problems despite their elaborate plans to avoid them. My turn came when our first Umbroller contractor could not meet his promised delivery dates despite protests that he had everything under control. As our purchase order cancellation dates approached, I began to work closely with this contractor to increase his daily output. What started as a short-term project to improve an inefficient production line became an around-the-clock project lasting several months. From that time on, I devoted a major portion of my time to operations problems. Be prepared to do the same, even though you work hard to avoid it. From my experiences, I found that operations tasks could be divided into three broad categories: materials and equipment, cost control, and people.

MATERIALS AND EQUIPMENT

Approximately 70 percent of the cost of goods sold is usually material and equipment expense. Most firms discover that over 50 percent of their sales dollars are tied up in these same expenditures. This means that effective control of this category is an important tool in stabilizing your new venture.

Decisions to purchase materials and equipment should depend directly on sales activity. Your order-entry system will be the first vital link in your operations information system. Production planning, in conjunction with marketing and sales input, should determine what tasks must be performed by purchasing and operations employees. Longer-range forecasts should influence factory layout and location. Make-or-buy, fixed-assets, and quality-control decisions will be natural byproducts of this same planning process. Your understanding of the interdependence of these variables will have an important impact on achieving the overall goal of stabilizing the operations function.

Order Entry

Order entry is the first step in delivering your product or service to your customers. An effective system will minimize internal costs, expedite processing, systematize planning, and provide each function with vital information to act upon.

Log each customer order separately and give it a control number. Establish a customer file for each regular account, and file the remaining ones under miscellaneous. Make a daily summary of order reports available to all department heads.

When these figures are tabulated by week, month, and quarter, important trends can be spotted that will be essential for your organization to adapt to the current buying activities of your customers. Your accountant should guide you in setting up a simple system. A note of caution: Although the order-entry system seems easy, it gives most new ventures fits, so do not treat it lightly. If the orders are not processed efficiently, virtually everything else will get out of control too.

Production Planning

Just as the production process should be geared to the inflow of purchase orders, so should the system for fulfilling customer orders be influenced by constraints on production. The first step is to set up effective communications between the marketing and operations departments so customer orders can be fulfilled in the most profitable manner. Flexible product specifications usually present excellent opportunities for the new venture to reduce costs and improve customer delivery performance. Over-specification for product performance, dimensions, styles, and delivery dates usually hamstring the new venture and create a profit drag. Be alert to this problem; most overspecification is very costly and due principally to inertia and established practices.

In 1973 we created an operations-marketing task force of three people to eliminate overspecifications from our product line. The results exceeded even our own optimistic expectations. Four Umbroller, five backpack, and six crib models were eliminated from the line, reducing our model numbers by 45 percent. Despite this drastic cut, our accountant projected little savings from these changes; however, substantial indirect cost reductions were achieved as several suppliers and part numbers were eliminated, raw material and work-in-process inventory were reduced, and deliveries and assembly-line efficiencies, now having fewer model numbers to contend with, improved. Creative production planning also uncovers substantial cost-savings opportunities by forcing other departments to provide wider latitude in product or service specifications.

Purchasing

Purchasing activity should be directly determined by production planning. The bulk of purchasing is with a few vendors, as a rule. This gives you an opportunity to tighten your cost structure without committing too much time to the effort. Although one hundred vendors supplied Cross River with stroller materials, only five accounted for 65 percent of our dollar purchases.

With these five, I concentrated on reducing product costs. A careful study of our aluminum costs, for example, indicated that minor variations in our purchasing behavior and fabricating processes could save 50 percent of our aluminum tubing expense and, therefore, 10 percent of our overall product cost. Interestingly, none of these savings came from purchasing larger volume; we had already capitalized on that rather obvious opportunity. The changes included buying mill lengths (in other words, purchasing the lengths most economic for their manufacturing system, not our own), cutting our own tubing (our supplier's cost system was based on feet produced per hour; tube cutting slowed down this rate and resulted in higher charges to us), and becoming a major off-season purchaser.

These savings resulted from our imagination and investigation, not from suggestions by the suppliers. You should try, as we did, to discover hidden cost-savings opportunities your vendors may never have considered. The high potential payoff more than warrants the effort.

Inventory Control

The production planning and purchasing functions must work together to control inventory. This is especially important because inventory tends to absorb cash, and, of course, the new company is almost always cash poor. Purchasing practices often contribute to this problem, for example, buying large quantities to qualify for discounts; this may not be wise, since the large expenditure places an increased burden on the company's cash flow. As a result, inventory levels must be carefully monitored by factory management and the entrepreneur.

The planning process should assist this effort by providing accurate sales and production forecasts so purchasing can minimize inventory levels. Marketing and sales can help by limiting product or service variations to minimize stock-keeping units and part numbers. Eliminating parts through an effective cost reduction program usually results in major inventory savings.

This function can be especially critical in seasonal or fashion-oriented businesses where obsolete inventories can become an enormous profit and cash drain. In new ventures, it is better to be cautious and risk being out of stock rather than face a potentially large inventory write down later. Unfortunately, this conservative suggestion conflicts with the entrepreneurial desire to satisfy customer requirements at all costs to insure growth. To guard against this aggressive tendency, remember that an inventory blunder or two may cost you your company.

At Cross River, my partner and I did, in fact, have an aggressive tendency to try to meet customer orders at all costs. This problem was compounded once when our fabric supplier offered us a particularly tempting discount if we committed to large production runs in advance. This lured us into over-committing to special patterns to qualify for the additional discounts and insure ourselves a total in-stock position on all fabrics. It took us two years and untold sleepless nights to work off the excess inventory, especially that of two patterns that soured in the marketplace. Your firm cannot afford to gamble too much on future purchases, even for substantial discounts. Avoid these advance commitments to raw material; they can lead to inventory imbalance and strangle your cash flow.

Factory Layout and Location

Factory location and layout form the cornerstone for the manufacturing system. The well-conceived layout saves innumerable direct and indirect costs. It can save square footage, prevent undue transportation expense, cut heat and power usage, reduce supervision costs, and increase the productivity of your employees. An efficient appearance seems to stimulate a faster work pace and higher-quality workmanship; likewise, it discourages sloppy and slow work. It encourages the creation of the stable operations system you must be so intent on developing.

Unnecessary movement and transportation of material can hinder effective production. It has been estimated that 50 percent of manufacturing costs relates to internal and external transportation expense. An effective layout can prevent this and help squeeze the substantial cost factor out of your operations expense.

Make or Buy: Marginal Returns

As stated earlier, most successful manufacturers started by subcontracting a major portion of their work. In trying to organize your business, you need all the help you can get from experienced contractors. If the outside price is close to your inside cost (including your factory overhead), buy the product or service outside to allow you to simplify your operations and concentrate on your other priorities.

A memorable example of my failing to follow this advice occurred when we brought the sewing of our stroller seat inhouse. Our contractor charged us 77 cents per delivered seat. We calculated our inhouse sewing costs at 35 cents per seat, a seemingly lower figure. With our full overhead accounted for, though, we would save just 7 cents apiece. With production of over 200,000 units per year at the time, we calculated a potential savings of $14,000 annually. Of course, the savings was essentially an illusion, since the basic expense was $140,000 and a $14,000 profit meant we were trying to earn a 10 percent manufacturing profit (not our skill) instead of pursuing more attractive marketing opportunities (our true skill). We did save the $14,000 and perhaps a little more, but the effort absorbed substantial management time and diverted us from exploiting better opportunities. It also expanded our labor force and plant facility, the cost of which was negligible in terms of money, but very real in terms of the time and energy expended. Watch out for these marginal returns in the operations system. The opportunities for them are abundant but can be extremely detrimental to your corporate growth and stability.

Fixed Assets and Other Anchors

Few areas are as conducive to empire building as operations. A huge modern plant will be a source of satisfaction to everyone. It will make your workers happier, your factory management prouder, your bankers more impressed, and—you can have it named after you! But your creaky old plant may cost just $1.25 per square foot while the new edifice runs over $4.50 per square foot. The down payment and subsequent mortgage payments may be staggering in the best of times and fatal in slow periods.

New plants should be postponed until enough cash is sitting idly in your local bank account or until your firm has substantial extra borrowing capacity. This does not usually occur until annual sales exceed ten million dollars. And even then, more companies are now leasing their facilities to improve their balance sheet and cash flow. Many corporations have identified their skills as non-asset management; Marriott Hotels, for example, has divested itself of its fixed assets, leased them back from financial institutions, and retained management contracts for the hotel facilities.

Another reason to avoid acquiring fixed assets is that the accelerating pace of social and technological change often outdates these assets rapidly. The perfect machine today may be obsolete in two years or the customer for your end product may have totally changed his or her purchasing requirements. Specially designed plant and equipment are particularly vulnerable to these changes. Consequently, the fixed assets that require one or two years of profitable use to justify their purchase may not only stretch your current cash position, but may also become useless because of changing technology or marketplace needs.

When fixed-asset purchases seem unavoidable, use imaginative purchasing approaches, since these can save your venture a fair amount of money. Usually, good planning gives you the time to locate a good buy, while poor planning invariably leads to needing it "right now" and contributes to a higher purchase cost. Good used equipment can be purchased at auctions or from equipment brokers. Several times at Cross River we bought used equipment at a fraction of the price of new equipment, and the older equipment worked just as well. More than a few times, however, we paid top dollar because we planned poorly and were forced to make immediate purchases.

Remember that just about everything bad can happen to fixed assets, from obsolescence to being the wrong selection. The cash saved by not making the purchase can have little go wrong with it.

You are taking enough risks; do not bet your company by committing your scarce cash resources on fixed assets. All too many entrepreneurial failures are caused by debts resulting from the overly aggressive acquisition of fixed assets. If you are at all in doubt about the purchase of a fixed asset, don't buy it!

Quality Control

Quality control is the stepchild of the operations system. It must be performed by operations people. Yet the function itself raises factory costs by requiring rework and the scrapping of parts and products. This can destroy a factory budget and bonus program. It makes operations employees police their own work and essentially function as a referee in their own game.

No truly good solution exists for this troubling problem. The best idea is to develop a market for your rejects; this way operations will not be charged for most of them and, likewise, not be tempted to cover up defects in quality. This also removes the temptation for you and your managers to "put them through" and compromise your quality standards. The use of outside contractors makes this task far easier (since they get penalized, not you). It also gives you time to establish adequate inspection standards without antagonizing your workers.

The best inspectors are usually older workers. They tend to be more thorough and more concerned about quality production. More than a few of these people have told me off as I tried to "put through" a defective item or two. And they were right. Employ this type of worker and you will undoubtedly be impressed by their performance. The best quality-control system will never accomplish what a few determined inspectors will. They will correct the sloppy workers as you cannot and keep the factory in relative harmony.

Retail Applications

Each of the above categories also applies directly to retail entrepreneurs. It is true that new venture retailers usually subordinate operations to other activities. They sometimes go too far in this direction, though, and pay too little heed to the procedural elements of their business.

Materials and equipment costs are usually over 50 percent of storekeeper expenses. Effective purchasing planning is required to assure that sufficient seasonal merchandise is available to capitalize on short periods of high consumer interest, yet at the same time protect against overstocking that can result in large inventory carry-overs to the next appropriate season. Carefully monitored order-entry and cash register receipts are vital links in determining which products are moving and which are slowing down. Quick reactions can permit suppliers to respond early to increased or decreased needs.

Retailers need to limit stock-keeping units every bit as much as manufacturers. Most first-time retailers tend to buy too broad a product line to encourage sales, yet do not stock their fastest moving items in enough depth. What they should concentrate on are the high-margin, fast-moving items that build traffic, turnover, and gross margin dollars.

In the infants' wear business, for example, many first-time hard-goods-oriented stores stock a wide variety of products. Competitive discounters stock a few, mark them up less than 50 percent, and build volume accordingly. Smart dealers have avoided direct competition with the discount trade by focusing on high-margin accessories that shoppers cannot get at the local discounters. They have cut back their hard-goods selection, put their dollars into accessory inventory, and built customer loyalty by providing much-needed accessories. Their hard-goods business has also increased, since many loyal accessory buyers buy their hard goods in the same stores because of convenience and store preference.

A major weakness of startup retailers is buying from those salespeople who call on them, rather than seeking out the most competitive lines. Many of your best potential sources will be complacent, uninterested in small-account business, and would just as soon have you buy from their competitors. However, despite their lack of enthusiasm for your business, many of these firms offer the best products, prices, and terms available in your market. You must use your imagination to convince them to deal with you.

An imaginative small-store owner in New York worked out a magnificent deal with Cross River through shrewdly evaluating our business needs. He recognized our tendency to discourage small-store business and to promote major account sales. He also noted, however, that our strollers could be reconditioned after they had become worn and that major accounts were unequipped to deal with this situation—but would like a repair station to refer their customers to. So, with this idea in mind, he approached me about setting up a New York City reconditioning station at his store.

Needless to say, I appreciated his suggestion. It solved a nagging consumer problem. We supplied him with an assortment of parts for reconditioning, and in appreciation for his services, we provided him with prompt delivery, the best prices, and accommodating payment terms. We also gave him all the write-in consumer business in his area, which broadened his customer base, increased consumer satisfaction in his area, and satisfied both of us. Small dealers are more flexible than larger accounts, and they can use this flexibility to interest major suppliers in doing business with them.

Store location and efficient layout are important in every new retail business. The key ingredient in retailing is location. This puts tremendous pressure on the startup entrepreneur to obtain scarce, expensive retail space. Without it, your new business must rely heavily on off-the-street traffic to compensate for not being located in a cluster of established stores with a loyal customer base.

Since 20 percent of your products will undoubtedly deliver 80 percent of your volume, it is generally better to acquire half the space needed in a good location rather than twice the space in a poor one. A survey of successful new startup retailers indicates a strong trend toward high-cost and well-located space rather than inexpensive and less-desired retail space.

Rather than investing heavily in store fixtures and equipment, select well-designed and packaged merchandise that will decorate and brighten your store. Careful control of unproductive costs, such as store decorations, will keep your break-even level down and prevent you from attempting to recover these dead costs by overpricing your retail merchandise.

Quality control can best be achieved by dealing with reputable suppliers. Guard against the tendency to buy from cheaper and less reliable sources. A solid company will take care of your customers if their product fails and assume legal responsibilities for defective products. Remember that your customers will associate poor products with your store, not the manufacturing source. A bad experience or two will antagonize the customer and, through word of mouth, hurt and possibly destroy your business. Keep this in mind when dealing with new products from unknown sources.

COST CONTROL

Cost control must be mastered to insure profitability and survival. Improved profitability comes either from sales increases or cost reductions. Sales growth strains your limited financial resources; cost reduction offers more attractive means of improving profits, since cost-reduced savings drop right to the bottom line.

In new ventures, cost-reduction opportunities are usually plentiful and often involve little or no cash investment. In many established companies, it is said that one dollar in cost savings is worth twenty in increased sales. Given the strain of growth on new-company resources, a dollar in cost savings is probably worth more than fifty in sales growth to a new firm.

Most entrepreneurs avoid concentrating on this high-potential profit area because it holds far less glamor than landing a new account or designing a new product. This lack of attention to cost control has often been the undoing of many an adventurous entrepreneur. One of the reasons surviving entrepreneurs tend to be of the less glamorous type is that the rather prosaic and unglamorous area of cost control demands just this sort of person. Without cost control, no secure foundation can be laid for orderly growth, profitability, and survival.

The reality of this was brought home to me when we added a twenty-thousand-dollar annual account on the same day that we eliminated four cents worth of parts from our stroller. The new account was a tremendous boost to the morale of our salesforce; the four-cent savings seemed an insignificant contribution even to our most dedicated operations people. Closer analysis, however, showed the cost savings to have far more importance to our company than acquiring the new account.

At the time we had a four-week backlog, so the new customer had more psychological than actual value to our firm. The elimination of four cents worth of parts, or eight hundred dollars of cost savings per month, could be initiated the next day. The cutback in parts purchasing was implemented the next week, and the actual cash savings occurred within three weeks.

As chief executive, you must create an atmosphere that encourages cost savings as much as sales increases. I did this by posting a graph showing that a one-cent cost savings was worth two thousand dollars per year and that it took a forty-thousand-dollar sales increase to equal the same bottom-line amount.

The following six suggestions should be borne in mind when beginning an effective cost control effort:

1. *It is easier to keep costs down than bring them down.* This suggestion should influence you not to rent the extra typewriter or hire the extra clerk, if it can be avoided at all. Much new venture expense is caused by adjustment for growth. If you can postpone the addition of overhead and people during a startup phase, you will often find your current staff sufficient after the transition period is over and things settle down; when the startup phase is over, the additional staff will be entrenched in their positions, even if they are no longer needed. A good way to avoid this problem is to give your regular staff a special bonus

for working extra hard during an expansionary period. This incentive will be appreciated, and far less costly than a permanent overhead increase.

2. *Costs increase in inverse proportion to effort.* Your visible attention to costs, more than anything else, is what will keep them under control. Your cost consciousness, or lack of it, will extend to your employees and vendors. My cheapness was infamous at Cross River. I picked up penny parts off the factory floor, raised hell about office expenses, grimaced when signing checks, jawboned with price-increasing vendors, and audited our payroll every week. As a result, our employees took pride in keeping costs down and were commended or reprimanded according to this standard.

3. *Cost control is more profitable during prosperity than during poor times.* Despite this rather obvious fact, most managers (including me) tend to do the reverse. It takes discipline not to relax your cost vigilance during good times. The most effective cost control programs usually occur in growth periods, when shrewd usage of materials, people, and equipment can avoid the need for more of the same to accommodate the higher sales levels created by growth. In periods of contraction, it is very hard to size down an operation and cut costs per unit at the same time.

4. *Costs tend to be variable going up and fixed coming down.* Some of this is due to laziness, but most is due to poor planning. Investments in people, equipment, leased space, and materials are often based on projected increases in sales. These items become hard to eliminate if volumes fail to materialize and these expenses must be pared down.

5. *In good times activities tend to proliferate.* This is the classic case of activities, or costs, expanding to fill space or your budget. The surest way to control costs is to eliminate marginal activities. It is far easier and less painful to eliminate an activity or two than to institute across-the-board 10 percent reductions in ten or fifteen departments.

6. *Elimination of activities and simplification of procedures.* As suggested above, it is usually easier to eliminate an activity

than to modify it. The 10-percent-across-the-board cost reduction programs hamstring useful efforts and have little impact on wasteful ones. Careful restructuring of jobs and departments to eliminate entire activities generally has better results. For example, a typical savings occurred when I eliminated the typing of customer statements by having overdue invoices copied and mailed instead. A time-consuming task became the routine job of copying and mailing a piece of paper.

One must continually guard against complication of procedures. Clerical and factory workers, lower management, and assorted support staff people have a habit of making their jobs unnecessarily complex and time-consuming. Extra reports, meetings, duplicated efforts, and extra expenditures will proliferate unless you keep close watch over them. Every once in a while you must reevaluate each department, identify its critical tasks, and eliminate the rest.

I have periodically reduced shipping and order-entry departments from four or five people to one or two by eliminating 75 percent of their procedures, reducing duplicated efforts, and straightening out the work flow. Yet the useless activities gradually cropped up again. This is an example of an aggravating but never-ending process of monitoring activities and eliminating waste.

Accurate Costs

Without an accurate set of numbers, your cost-cutting efforts will be in vain. Make sure you establish correct costs for each activity from advertising to production. A precise bill of materials, reliable labor standards, and accurate overhead cost reports should form the basis for determining what are your best potential cost-cutting targets. Very few entrepreneurial ventures have this data, since most new venture people feel more comfortable shooting from the hip. Make yourself the exception and a number of glaring cost overruns will be obvious at first glance. Accountants love to work with small business people interested in accurate costs; they will provide all the help and moral support you require.

Summary

Effective cost cutting must start with your dedication and example. No one else in your firm will have the incentive to do so: cost-reducing activities tend to create more work for the remaining employees, eliminate pleasant but useless frills, and instill a more austere atmosphere.

Employees have a definite interest in blunting your efforts and will do so unless you offer them incentives to cooperate with you. Remember that most of your employees do not share your concerns, since they do not hold stock in your company. Unless you put them on equal footing with you, do not expect them to support your objectives with equal vigor. Your best hope is to provide them with a reward system (both financial and personal) for contributing to your cost-control efforts. If you can succeed in that, you will have done far better than most entrepreneurs.

PEOPLE

Plant Management

Because of the special requirements of an operations startup, your first plant or store manager will have a number of non-recurring problems. He or she must establish and organize your first facility, design the layout, develop bills of material (a list of material costs for each product), set standards for employee hiring, and implement a number of other startup programs. In addition, this manager must cope with the financial pressures created by new venture cash flow constraints, limited capital budgets, and poor forecasting information. This is a far harder task than maintaining an ongoing store or plant facility.

The best operations managers have a tough—but limited—perspective. Your company needs this administrative discipline. Yet these people often have an extremely difficult time dealing with the chaotic circumstances of new venture life. They are not prepared for suppliers cutting the firm off, high absenteeism, and chaotic production planning resulting from poor marketing information.

The best job candidates will have had some experience managing a small-company facility. Any new-company startup experience would be an invaluable asset. The plant manager should ideally be in his or her late thirties or forties, if not older. The unwieldy nature of operations requires a mature individual.

You must work closely with your operations manager. Plant people pride themselves on their toughness. They often speak in military imagery and live out Patton or John Wayne fantasies. Most of them will be unpleasantly surprised by their inclination to panic when confronted with the chaos and pressures of new venture life. You must help them preserve their egos and self-confidence during their trial by fire, or they will wither away under the pressure. I have witnessed this disintegration process, and it was deadly to both the company and the individual. The tough-guy pose depends on a structure and organization which are already firmly in place. Without it, these people often become lost when they confront genuine enemies and not paper tigers.

Supervisors

Good supervisors are hard to develop but even more difficult to hire from the outside. The most stable performers tend to be homegrown and their promotion gives a powerful incentive to your other workers. But, perhaps more significantly, it is very hard to attract good first-line supervisors from other companies, since their current employers value and pay them so well that you can rarely lure them away. The ones you can attract are generally less competent and usually will have a negative effect on your fledgling organization. This is an especially aggravating problem because good first-line supervisors can be helpful in training and guiding the many new factory or clerical workers of a startup venture. At least in mature companies certain factory workers have substantial experience, feel comfortable in the work environment, and can help train and stabilize new employees.

The most effective approach seems to be to select potential supervisors from among your best factory workers. Do not, however, give them too much responsibility too quickly, or they may collapse under the increased pressures. Production people tend to be like good wine—they need aging to reach their best performance levels.

Factory and Clerical Workers

The agony of dealing with factory and clerical workers is almost unimaginable. I have received birthday cakes, home-cooked lunches, propositions, honors, thrown knives, flat tires, headaches, and a few punches. While most of these people live quite stable and normal lives, just enough of them do not to make you think your entire company is filled with lunatics. It is important to establish some distance between yourself and your workers, or you will lose all objectivity in running the firm. This is much easier said than done.

The first goal in hiring factory or clerical people should be to seek stable individuals. Only then can you evaluate them in terms of speed, quality, and attendance. From the outset, you should accept a high failure rate in the hiring process. It is better to try more workers and weed out the poor ones quickly than to attempt to be more selective initially and slow to terminate the ineffective ones. It is extremely difficult to tell from an interview, reference check, or other test who will work out and who will not.

My experience has been that the best workers tend to be over thirty, married with no children, and have never received welfare or other government assistance. Often, they are entering the labor market because they have just moved into the neighborhood or because the support of their family requires them to take a job. Another good prospect is someone seeking work because their last company closed down or left the area. These people can be real jewels in the long run. The worst candidates tend to be those with active problems (recent divorce, custody battles, and the like), women with three or more young children, and antagonistic individuals.

If an individual seems like a good candidate, tell him or her that during the first week he or she must work a complete forty-hour week or be automatically terminated. This demand often uncovers innumerable problems about individuals; they will describe a host of reasons why perfect attendance is impossible during the first week. My response is that once they have cleaned up their problems, they can call me for another interview. Do not give them a delayed starting date.

Over 50 percent of the people I have told this to never called back. I suspect that most of them were put off by our attendance policy and simply withdrew themselves from consideration. The ones willing to start under these conditions generally performed well and were pleased with being given a specific standard to meet.

During the first week make a careful check of the quantity produced and quality of performance. Generally a one-day check will give you a good idea whether a worker will work out or not; a one-week check is almost always enough. If the worker is marginal, let him or her go, and seek a new worker. Compromising your standards, no matter how pressing your production schedule, will have a disastrous effect on the quality and productivity of your work force.

The final decision to hire should be made after a trial period of thirty days. If the worker seems satisfactory at this point, the probability is very high that he or she will perform well over the long run. This system will not be equitable each time, but, by giving applicants a trial run, your record of fairness will be better than if you had selected fewer people. Judging entry-level employees too individually, without seeing their actual work, tends to promote discriminatory practices relating to age, sex, and race.

UNIONS: THE ENTREPRENEURIAL NIGHTMARE

Sooner or later the unions will get you. Contrary to entrepreneurial fears, unions do not want to run your business.

In fact they only want to collect dues from your employees and offer them reasonable representation at the bargaining table. Union leaders are often quite sympathetic with small-company problems and are not inclined to disturb new ventures.

In the small-company environment unions can act as a stabilizing element. As a practice, they usually install department stewards who serve as focal points for the various minor problems your supervisors are continually plagued with. They generally inform management of problems before they get out of control and provide a systematic means of coping with them. Unions also absorb a substantial amount of the worker hostility once directed toward you; much of the petty complaining that used to provoke your nonunion managers is now directed toward union personnel. Finally, unions eliminate the entrepreneur's self-deceptive feeling that "we are all one happy family."

The reasons for opposing unionization are well known. You must, however, get on with your business and not spend too much time or energy on this problem. A nonunion company is generally better for all concerned until a firm has more than five hundred employees. As a practical matter, there is not much need to worry; by the time unions can become a genuine threat to new ventures, the company has usually grown to such a size that the founders have sold out and are long gone.

If your employees wish to bring in a union, make sure it is clean and then give them your blessing to put the matter to an immediate vote. If the employees recognize your willingness to consider the issue openly, they may find this the most persuasive reason for voting against the union.

I began my career fighting off the UAW, Teamsters, and IUE. It was a terrible waste of effort and resources. When my first company was finally organized, all the union did was collect dues, enforce a more uniform set of work rules (which only helped the company), and serve as an outlet for the workers' anxieties. Their business agent was a reasonable person and the wage increases were less than we would have voluntarily offered. Try to control your emotional reaction in this area and you will improve your chances for remaining a nonunion company. And if your firm does unionize, a more even-tempered attitude will keep the situation under control.

A FINAL NOTE: PERSONAL TRAINING

Unlike most functions, operations skills lend themselves to rapid study. Work flow, layout, site selection, and material control are issues subject to specific criteria for sound decision making. If possible, attend one local business school course in operations management. I took an evening course in industrial management at Columbia University and it assisted me greatly in laying out my Cross River plants. Our methods of line balancing, materials flow, and our raw material inventory systems came right out of my textbook and course readings. No other business area is so readily learned from an academic course, so take advantage of this opportunity if you can.

Professionals
and the Business
Environment

New ventures seem to have all the problems of General Motors without the resources to cope with them. The appropriate professionals can help a new firm cut through these difficulties. They can define the most important problems and opportunities your firm will confront as it matures.

Unfortunately, the best professionals seem to charge the highest hourly rates. In the long run, though, the best ones are usually the least expensive because they work quickly, accurately, and have an uncanny knack of being able to resolve problems before they get out of control.

Seek the finest professionals you can interest in your fledgling enterprise. Remember that these people will charge high hourly rates precisely because so many companies stand to benefit from their services. As a result, you must convince them to work with your venture, as only mediocre professionals will usually bother soliciting your business.

LAWYERS

Most effective corporate attorneys are cautious, worldly, conservative people. They view their primary role as preventing problems from occurring rather than engaging in legal battles or maneuvers. These individuals usually have a keen business sense. They have better instincts than their clients for negotiations, priorities, and long-term solutions. They are usually not as good at understanding day-to-day business activities, marketing problems, or production requirements. However, they are occasionally gifted in finance, public relations, and in using the old-boy network. Use your lawyer for his or her strengths, avoid weaknesses, and you will have an invaluable asset to your management team.

At Cross River, law firms not only resolved innumerable legal entanglements but also introduced us to catalog showroom sales representatives who opened this distribution network for our company. Within two years, over 20 percent of our sales came from catalog showroom customers. In another instance, our lawyers recommended an investor to underwrite a second mortgage for a new plant facility. Each suggestion was made in the midst of other conversations, yet despite the casual nature of their assistance, these ideas increased our sales by over one million dollars and saved us numerous costs in our plant acquisition.

You need a law firm with an excellent reputation precisely because your company has none. General Motors may not need to work with a prestigious firm, but your venture does. If possible, avoid unknown firms regardless of the financial incentives to do otherwise. A well-connected law firm can save you substantial costs, influence otherwise uninterested outsiders to deal with your venture, and guide you as effectively as they have other clients. If you cannot follow this advice at first because of other commitments, do so as soon as possible.

Normally, the senior partner assigned to your account is the crucial individual for you to evaluate. As a chief executive, you will be called upon to make eight to ten major decisions per year. Corporate counsel should be involved in at least half of them. As a consequence, you should select your counsel just as carefully as you would your two or three key managers.

Most entrepreneurs give little thought to this selection process, though they often have the leanest of managements and should therefore rely even more heavily on corporate counsel for advice. The practical consequence of this is that most entrepreneurs rarely hire good counsel and usually ignore their advice in any event.

You can improve your odds for success by avoiding this pitfall and giving the legal selection process your attention. Senior law partners spend most of their time on significant corporate issues because of their professional interests, their power within the firm to get favored assignments, and their high hourly rates. As a consequence they will have considerable experience in many of the areas you will be untutored in. Private placements, stock issues, mergers, acquisitions, negotiations, litigation settlements, and patent problems are frequent occurrences for them, whereas they will be rarities for you. Consider the advantages of using this wisdom and experience before dismissing the law firm decision as unimportant. You do not always need to follow their advice, but you should at least listen to it.

The junior partners assigned to your account will do the daily routine work, and as a result may be almost as important to your company as their seniors. Most lawyers have a sound tendency to seek the advice of others. Younger attorneys are more apt not to do this, so make sure junior partners seek the advice of others—especially of the senior partner.

The law-firm-selection process should emphasize the quality of the senior and junior lawyers assigned to your account and the prestige and influence of the law firm itself. If your first choice is not interested in working with your venture, seek the next best firm and keep trying until one is committed to work with you. When your back is to the wall it is often the lawyers who must save you. Be sure these people will hold up under fire and are the ones you want with you in your foxhole.

ACCOUNTANTS

Accountants should not be treated lightly as bookkeepers or number-tumblers. Nor should they rule your company. The selection of an accounting firm is not as critical as that of the law firm, though some would argue to the contrary. Accountants have a less significant effect on your business because their job does not involve them in as many corporate decisions.

Your accounting firm will audit your books, sign their name to your financial statements, and thereby contribute to or detract from your corporate credibility. In new ventures, the verbal recommendations of your outside accountants can have a major effect on the credit lines vendors extend to your firm. For this reason alone it is usually advisable to select a Big Eight firm, since they are well known and respected in the credit community.

Big Eight accountants are also well connected with potential money sources. Like your lawyers, your accountants can put you in touch with excellent people and companies that will otherwise remain unknown to you. Our Cross River accountants saved us countless dollars by introducing us to one of their clients who carried junked equipment, which we then bought from them for a fraction of its original cost. Another time, they recommended an excellent subcontractor, a sewing machine foreman, and a good product design firm. Each of these suggestions was made during conversations on other subjects, but each made a contribution to our corporate well-being and profitability.

Your selection procedure should be similar to the one followed in selecting your law firm. Any Big Eight firm should be satisfactory; if none will work with you in your startup phase, use a good local firm until you can attract a Big Eight member at a later date. The senior accountant is the key person to evaluate, since this is the person who will be called upon to recommend your creditworthiness to your prospective suppliers, lenders, and investors. Your accountant must have the business savvy to sell these people on your stability and financial potential. He or she must be imaginative enough to work *with* the numbers rather than be ruled or intimidated by them, otherwise your creditors will not be convinced to grant your company the credit it will require. The accountant should also be involved with other small-business clients, since, as I have suggested in earlier chapters, big business methods will sink your venture. A senior accountant with selling savvy and small-business experience can be invaluable to your credit-hungry company.

The junior accountants often seem far less important, since they rarely give credit references and their work principally consists of tallying up the numbers for the senior accountant. The accounting profession also tends to be more hierarchical than the legal one, so these people are even less visible to outsiders than young lawyers. However, your junior accountants can provide invaluable practical insights into running your business. The junior partner assigned to Cross River was my best sounding board for internal financial decisions. When we had financial problems, he was the one I sought to assist me in unraveling the mysteries. If you seek junior people's advice and give them the confidence and respect they merit, they will contribute to the stability and profitability of your company.

CONSULTANTS

As an entrepreneur, it is important to solicit advice from people more experienced than yourself. These individuals need not be associated with your own company, your law or accounting firm, or a large consulting organization. In fact, the best advisers are often independent consultants not associated with a large firm.

At Cross River, for example, I received helpful advice from a one-man firm who came for a week and stayed for eight months to organize and manage our main plant. His practical experience as a Whirlpool plant manager, and with small-company assignments such as our own, proved invaluable to us. Our experience with several major consulting firms, on the other hand, was disastrous. They billed us three times their initial estimates and left us with inconclusive reports.

A new venture should require its consultants to be able to translate their advice into concrete improvements. Our consultant implemented cost and systems improvements within his first days on the job, and positive results were felt within a week. Similarly, the ineffectiveness of the major consulting firms surfaced immediately. In the small-company environment, consultants should be able to make immediate improvements, or they are the wrong people for the job. When interviewing prospective consultants, observe the individual's sense for changing specific elements in your company. His or her interest in developing bills of material, plant layouts, identifying new customer prospects, or revising collection procedures is evidence that he or she is likely to be successful in a small firm. Broad projects such as developing marketing plans, making your plant more efficient, or revising your accounting system are signs of a potentially ineffective and disappointing consulting relationship. Good small-company consultants should be able to make several quick fixes to save your company money. If they are unable to do so, they are probably the wrong people for your business.

THE INTIMIDATED PROFESSIONAL

Entrepreneurs can usually beat other professionals in an argument. Normally, they are more persuasive individuals—and, after all, the entrepreneur is the boss and pays the bills. Professionals usually dislike being put through the wringer and, as a result, often capitulate too easily, even on important issues.

It is therefore up to you to maintain an open atmosphere and prevent this tendency to browbeat from infecting your professional relationships. You must avoid the entrepreneurial impulse to execute the messengers of bad tidings, or you will not hear about potential calamities far enough in advance to prevent them. New venture professionals are often the most reliable barometers of problems and opportunities. Nurture their candor and commitment to your firm and you will be rewarded many times over. They can only assist you if they are permitted to air their views candidly. They are not always right, but, often enough, they are.

THE COMMUNITY AND OTHER
EGO-BOOSTING ACTIVITIES

The best service you can provide your community at the outset is to build a stable company. This will create employment, provide local suppliers with new business, and stand as a symbol of local economic opportunity. Speeches, Rotary Club memberships, United Fund Committees, and Blue Ribbon panels will only undermine your managerial effectiveness by deflecting your attention from your new business. There will be time enough for this ego boosting later in your career. It has been fatal to many entrepreneurs. Don't let it happen to you.

GOVERNMENT AGENCIES

The Time Sponges

Aside from the SBA, virtually every other government agency will be unhelpful at best, and a threat to your corporate existence at worst. The agencies that would seem helpful in economic development or exporting are in fact of little use to the small company. The entrepreneur simply does not have the time, money, or energy to seek the assistance of these organizations, since they will at most deliver marginal results.

My favorite example occurred with the New York State Commission for Export Assistance. I replied to a magazine ad promising free help in export assistance. A civil servant called and arranged a meeting at our mutual convenience, at which he spent the first thirty minutes filling out his call report. After another hour of wasted discussion, I was placed on their mailing list for foreign companies interested in importing American products. After reading their bulletins, mailing inquiries that were never answered, and getting generally frustrated with the whole situation, I requested that my name be removed from the list. Out came my friend again for a debriefing session. After he had harangued me for an hour and a half, I finally agreed to attend a seminar.

The seminar leader rattled on for several hours, speaking in generalities about the benefits of exporting. He concluded with the idea that West Germany and Japan were good potential markets—something a casual newspaper reader could have figured out. But when I asked him for specific information about letters of credit and customs duties, he told me that these were technicalities and not his concern. He was polite, thoughtful, yet a definite example of the time sponge. This experience was repeated several times, until I learned to avoid government agencies entirely.

The Adversary Agencies

The other governmental agencies are, in fact, your hereditary enemies. These agencies are not only time sponges, which is bad enough, but they can bankrupt your firm, close your factories, fine you, and put you in jail. The government workers who are the instruments of these agencies tend to be disarmingly courteous and helpful people. They generally make every effort to be equitable; being with them, though, is like trying to remain at ease in a lion's cage—the beasts may be mild-mannered, but you know they can maul you at will!

The following is a brief list of the more dangerous agencies. The first is the *Internal Revenue Service*. This agency is definitely King of the Jungle. Pay them on time—they can padlock your corporate door, make you personally liable for deficient payments, and put you in jail. The most common way of inviting trouble is not to pay employee withholding taxes on time. This creates difficulty because the withheld amounts can accumulate so quickly. Withholding taxes represent a large portion of your cost of goods sold, and a few weeks of not paying them can disrupt your cash flow and make catch-up efforts almost impossible. Discipline yourself to pay these bills on time despite the fact the payments are voluntarily deposited with your bank, and no credit manager will call you as a reminder. Since their power of expropriation puts them ahead of all other creditors, the IRS is reluctant to work with new companies. Nonpayment of these taxes also puts you in default of virtually any commercial lending agreement, which further strengthens the IRS's position. Failure to pay income tax on earnings is a less serious problem because, if you are making money, most banks will loan you sufficient funds to make this type of payment.

If you get behind in your withholding taxes, do not make a clean breast of it, no matter how satisfying the confession would be or how much your accountant wants you to make it. Instead, pay all current obligations to the IRS on time. Then amortize your indebtedness over a three-month period (or over six months, if necessary), making the extra payments weekly—not biweekly or monthly.

This strategy is necessary because your IRS agent must start the clock as soon as he or she knows you are in default. If you bring the matter to the agent's attention, it just increases the pressure on your payment schedule. Once you are found in default, the IRS agent must make an arbitrary assessment of your ability to pay. If you have already implemented a corrective plan, you will have demonstrated your willingness and ability to pay. The entrepreneur who shows the discipline for self-corrective action will probably be a better risk—the IRS agent knows this from experience—and is more likely to receive a liberal payment schedule.

A *state sales tax agency* presents the retailer with as many dangers as the IRS does for all firms. All IRS warnings and recommendations apply to these agencies.

Labor-related agencies have proliferated in recent years. They inspect facilities for safety, check your wage-payment schedules for compliance with various laws, and referee union-related activities. Dealing with these organizations is generally time-consuming and a nuisance. Most of the inspectors are pleasant, affable people with time on their hands, involved as they are in a moderately patronage-prone, featherbedded job. However, if you try to get tough with them, they can get even tougher with you.

You can get into trouble with overtime payments, age-sex-race discrimination, NLRB (union organizing), and OSHA (safety regulations). The best way to cope with these people is to listen to them, not argue, and comply as promptly as possible with their recommendations. To do otherwise is to encourage time-wasting feuds in which they will always have the upper hand.

Since most small-business people have a not entirely unjustified reputation for fatheadedness, stubbornness, and the like, make a point of being rational when speaking with civil servants or other governmental representatives. On the whole, the inspectors tend to be trivial and petty, but very few are venal or carry grudges. Do not succumb to filibustering about the evils of government and you will succeed more easily in ridding yourself of these well-meaning pests.

Conclusion

WHEN TO GET OUT

Your venture will be a going concern when it can operate profitably without your direct involvement. Your company will achieve maturity when a professional manager can run it successfully.

This definition deliberately excludes businesses that depend on personal skills of the entrepreneur. It also excludes companies subsidized by the entrepreneur through family, personal, or other means.

Once your firm passes this test, you must decide whether to stay on as an executive-curator or leave by selling out. The choice is that simple and direct. At this point, entrepreneurial instincts and abilities can become hazardous to corporate health. Entrepreneurs who remain with their firms habitually practice brinksmanship and wreak havoc to make themselves feel invaluable again.

One of your toughest jobs will be to recognize when this point has been reached. Founders avoid this recognition because they naturally find it hard to confront their own diminished importance. After all, the true entrepreneurial high comes from the struggle, not the success. Yet, as in raising children, you must let the company evolve and mature, or its growth will be stunted and your relationship to it permanently harmed and perhaps even ruined.

This loss will occur only if you are successful in launching your company by meeting your primary objective of creating a stable economic entity. This is the true irony of entrepreneurial life. Some of the early warning signs are:

1. Reminiscing about the good old days with early employees
2. Customers casually referring to your company as an established part of the industry
3. Fewer suppliers demanding financial statements
4. Your personal guarantee becoming less of an issue in financial transactions

It is crucial for you to recognize this moment in your company's life cycle. Many emerging companies have reached the going-concern stage only to be unraveled and often destroyed unconsciously by founders seeking the good old days when they were indispensable to the firm. Prepare for this situation in advance; do not let all your effort and investment go to waste. Remember that successful gamblers make their money by knowing when to get out of the game.

Appendix

Most business reports are cumbersome rather than action oriented. They often serve as a means to cover the writer's flanks rather than to promote effective decision making. As a result, most entrepreneurs shy away from these documents entirely. This is an overreaction, since new ventures need current information to evaluate the state of their business, identify new trends, and make effective decisions.

The following four reports are simple and action oriented.

FINANCIAL REPORT

	This Year	Year Ago		Variance	
Accounts Receivable	_____	_____	$ _____	%	_____
Bank Balance	_____	_____	_____		_____
Total Current Assets*	_____	_____	_____		_____
Accounts Payable	_____	_____	_____		_____
Loans	_____	_____	_____		_____
Total Current Liabilities*	_____	_____	_____		_____
Spread between Current Assets and Liabilities	_____	_____	_____		_____
Orders in House	_____	_____	_____		_____
Payroll:					
Last Weeks—$	_____	_____	_____		_____
Employees—#	_____	_____	_____		_____
Other†	_____	_____	_____		_____

* Current asset and liability figures purposefully exclude items that are not easily converted into cash, such as inventory and prepaid expenses.

† This category is used to track certain prominent short-term items such as new-product production or sales. This portion of the report should be used sparingly so the document does not become unwieldy.

They have served me well in managing my own ventures. Each chart is relatively easy to keep updated. The key-account file requires the most attention, yet these charts should justify your efforts because they provide some of the most useful information for the new enterprise.

SALES REPORT

Month	This Year	Year Ago	Variance $	Variance %
1				
2				
3				
4				
5				
6				
7				
8				
9				
10				
11				
12				
13				
14				
15				
16				
17				
18				
19				
20				
21				
22				
23				
24				
25				
26				
27				
28				
29				
30				
31				

Month to Date   ————   ————   ————   ————
January
February
March
April
May
June
July
August
September
October
November
December
Year to Date

KEY-ACCOUNT FILE*

Name, Address, Phone Number: _____

Annual Corporate Sales: _____
Annual Department or Division Sales: _____
NYSE Listed: _____   D&B Rating: _____
Annual Report included: _____
Chief Competitors: _____
    (to your firm) _____
Chief Competitors: _____
    (for them) _____
Major influences on their decision making: _____
_____
_____
_____

Corporate, department strategies applicable to your business: _____
_____
_____
_____

Special issues, events, or other: _____
_____
_____
_____

Key contacts at this company: _____
_____
_____
_____

* As pointed out in the earlier chapters, this form should be used for all the important companies with which your business deals. This should include, among others, major customers (especially the Top 200 referred to in the sales chapter), vendors, and lenders.

PRODUCTION REPORT: UNITS PRODUCED*

Month	THIS YEAR Product A	Product B	Total	LAST YEAR Product A	Product B	Total	VARIANCE Product A	Product B	Total
1									
2									
3									
4									
5									
6									
7									
8									
9									
10									
11									
12									
13									
14									
15									
16									
17									
18									
19									
20									
21									

22

23

24

25

26

27

28

29

30

31

Month to Date

January

February

March

April

May

June

July

August

September

October

November

December

Year to Date

* This report is useful only for manufacturing companies.

Related Readings

The four books listed below have been the most useful to me in my entrepreneurial career. On that basis, I recommend them to you.

Drucker, Peter F. *Managing for Results*. New York: Harper & Row, 1964. This landmark work is required reading for all my managerial employees. The insights are so fresh that I reread this book every six months or so. At a minimum, read the first chapter, "Business Realities." After that, I challenge you to try *not* to complete the book.

Townsend, Robert. *Up the Organization*. Greenwich, Connecticut: Fawcett, 1971. Townsend deflates much business mythology. His emphasis is on justice, fun, and excellence, and his humor never flags. A remarkable achievement.

McGregor, Douglas. *The Human Side of Enterprise*. New York: McGraw-Hill, 1960. One of the earliest, and still perhaps the best, works on the people side of business.

Drucker, Peter F. *Management*. New York: Harper & Row, 1974. A later and more learned version of *Managing for Results*. New insights and fresh thinking throughout.

Index